Table of Contents

Today's Globalization

Project South: Institute for the Elimination of Poverty & Genocide

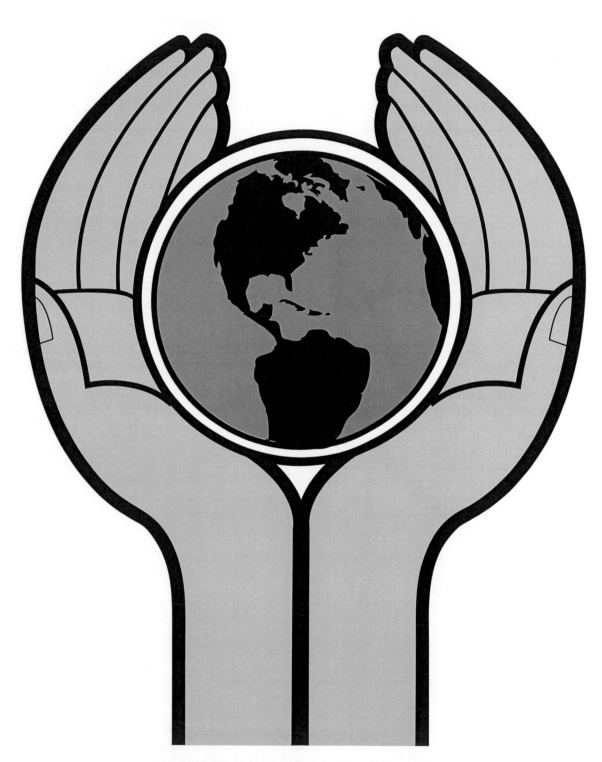

Project South: Institute for the Elimination of Poverty & Genocide

What is Project South?

Project South: Institute for the Elimination of Poverty and Genocide is a Southern based, leadership development organization creating spaces for movement building. We work with communities pushed forward by the struggle to strengthen leadership and provide popular political and economic education for personal and social transformation. We build relationships with organizations and networks across the US and global South to inform and connect to our local work.

Incorporated in 1991, Project South was formed to meet the need for accessible education about the history of African Americans and the South's strategic relationship to the nation as a whole. After organizing several summits of the Southern region of the Up and Out of Poverty Now! Campaign — a coalition of homeless unions, anti-hunger and welfare-rights organizations — the leadership of the Campaign identified the continuous need for accessible political education. Project South took on that role.

In 1997 we made the organizational commitment to develop "indigenous" popular educators — people who develop and use popular education and action research as tools to build their own communities and organizations. Since then, we have developed a number of workshops, tools, and methods to make vital information about changes in economic trends and public policy more accessible to low-income communities — the communities most negatively impacted by regressive policy and economic inequality.

Strategically located in the Southeastern United States, Project South works primarily with groups in the state of Georgia and throughout the Southeast (including Washington, DC). We also do work on the national and international levels. Our constituency is made up of students, youth, cultural workers, scholar-activists, welfare recipients, community-based groups, and workers' organizations — primarily grassroots groups based in low-income/working class communities and communities of color.

Project South Staff: 2005

Project South: Institute for the Elimination of Poverty & Genocide

How do I use this Toolkit in my work?
Today's Globalization Toolkit Tells a Story

Over the last 500 years our world and its many communities have become increasingly connected. Often times this "globalization" of our world has been driven by social and economic expansion and exploitation. The idea and ideology of capitalism was born in Europe but has become a dominant global force, ever-changing with the historical moment in which it operates. Within this context people in communities have stood together to challenge the many faces of oppression and injustice that have emerged. This toolkit covers: some of the changes that have occurred throughout this history, how today's globalization differs, and how people in community can organize themselves to effectively seek justice and human rights.

Poor People's Day: Georgia State Capitol 2005

How to Use this Toolkit

This toolkit was designed for:
Grassroots organizations, local community members, scholar-activists, students, young people, and anyone else who wants to learn more about globalization and provide a workshop for on how the issues of Globalization affect us in our local communities.

We call Today's Globalization a "toolkit" because its like a bag of tools that you can use to help build your understanding of globalization.

Included within this toolkit are several different resources designed to give you more information about Today's Globalization. We include a Workshop Curriculum that was designed by the staff of Project South. This toolkit and all of Project South's publications are informed by our work with many different organizations across the country.

An Analysis of Globalization Today

Project South: Institute for the Elimination of Poverty & Genocide

Globalization in World History

GLOBALIZATION IS NOT NEW

Globalization of the capitalist world economy over the last 500+ years has gone through three stages of development:

1) The Mercantile age
2) The modern Industrial-Financial age
3) Today's Electronic age.

British Colonial forces attack Zulu warriors

What remains essential to the capitalist global economy in all ages is that it is a market economy. Labor is a commodity that produces new value, and the drive for maximum profits through production and sale of goods and services – commodities – in the market. The 20th century spans the final expansion and end of the Industrial-Financial age and the emergence of the Electronic age in the last two decades of the century.

1973 Mohawk Nation: woodcut by Bruce Carter

We examine the interrelationship between the interests of economic elites in these stages, the popular movements and demands of the people most marginalized, and the political struggles and policy outcomes.

What is new about this Historical Moment?

The Power of Global Corporations

Today's global corporations are, in many ways, more powerful than nation states. Through policies such as NAFTA and associations like the WTO, corporations have more power to assert their interests (maximum profits) than any other moment in history.

Photo by Dustin Ross: RNC Convention

The idea of "Neoliberalism"

Neoliberal (reactionary and regressive) policies - used throughout the developing world for decades and more recently implemented in the US. These policies maximize profits for global corporations within the context of political control (reform, repression) at home and abroad.

1. Race to the bottom: automation, downsizing, competition among workers around the world, labor and environmental protections eroded, rise of sweatshops, decline in wages and living standards

2. Privatization of the public sector (government services, education, health care, welfare, prisons, etc.)

3. Social contract broken, safety net shredded, welfare recipients in labor force increases the supply of cheap labor, poverty - especially child poverty - deepens

4. The gap between rich and poor widens - greater polarization of wealth, income, and poverty

5. Repression Increases - prison industrial complex, incarceration, militarization, death penalty, police brutality, etc.

Electronics & New Technologies for Global Capitalism

Information is a highly valued commodity. Knowledge becomes intellectual property; computers - through digitalization - rapidly replace both physical and mental human labor. Technologies of communication and transportation bind the world more tightly - instantaneous flows of capital, enhanced flows of goods & services, and migration of labor. With electronics we produce more with less labor power. Workers (in manufacturing and services) are not needed in production and distribution of goods and services, so they have fewer wages to buy back the things they need. Workers are in crisis, and markets shrink.

In short: The welfare state is replaced by growing police state policies; global corporations reap record profits and place their 'right to profit' over the Human Rights of most people, while wealth, resources and income are more unequally distributed than ever!

However, popular movements against today's top-down (corporate) globalization and neoliberal policies are increasing and connecting to each other.

Three Key Moments for Globalization in US History

1.

(1929-1945) Great Depression - End of WWII - Beginning Welfare State Reform:
In the Industrial-Financial stage of capitalism, the New Deal ushers in America's welfare state (Social Security Act 1935) as a social contract with the more privileged section of industrial and middle class, mostly white workers. The New Deal is a response to the militant demands of a powerful industrial trade union movement and the efforts of the economic elite & corporations to bring the country out of the Great Depression and prepare for war production. Multinational corporations are becoming a powerful force in the world economy, but the nation state remains a key actor on the world stage.

2.

(1945-1970's) Post-WWII Expanding Economy & Welfare State Reform
This expansion of industry and finance capital through multinational corporations sets the basis for the powerful social movements of the 1950's-70's (civil rights, women, anti-war, ethnic/racial, gay rights, environmental, national liberation) for inclusion into American society and/or the global economy. In response, the US "war on poverty" expands the social contract of the welfare state to include people of color and the poor, though women of color and their children are stigmatized even within the expanded welfare state. Globally, their counterparts in the developing world do not benefit from this economic expansion. The Bretton Woods financial institutions (World Bank, International Monetary Fund, & General Agreement on Tariffs and Trade) impose harsh policies of structural adjustment programs (SAPs) on the people of the developing world that demand government funds be spent on maximizing profits from production for export and paying down the growing debt to the IMF and WB, rather than securing the social well-being of the people (food security, housing, health care, sanitation - including clean water, education, etc.).

3.

(1980's-2005) The Electronic Age - Global Corporations Rule & Neoliberalism:
The electronics revolution (computers, robotics, automation) in production and distribution of goods and services transforms the economic expansion of the 1990's into a contraction for working and middle class people in the developing and developed countries in the new global economy. Global corporations assume greater and greater power. They establish new global policies and institutions such as NAFTA (North American Free Trade Agreement), new GATT policies, and the WTO (World Trade Organization) that transcend nation state borders and replace national and local law with new global policies.

Building today's global movement for economic & social justice
Understanding the World as it Really is & as it is Becoming

By Jerome Scott & Walda Katz-Fishman

"At the risk of seeming ridiculous, let me say that the true revolutionary is guided by a great feeling of love. ... [We] must idealize this love of the people, the most sacred cause, and make it one and indivisible."
-Che Guevara from *Socialism and Man*, 1965

Building blocks for our movement
Three essential building blocks for our economic and social justice movement are critical consciousness, vision, and strategy - CVS. Critical consciousness is our understanding of how the world works and our place in it, including our sense of history. Vision is the big and bold picture we create of the world we want for our families, our communities and our planet. Strategy is the plan we collectively make to change the world in which we live into the world we envision. The movement's emerging leaders must know these building blocks well and use them to ground and give direction to our movement.

Questions we must answer
To build today's global movement for economic and social justice we must be clear about the answers to the following three questions. 1. What is today's globalization and what does it mean? 2. Why do we need a global movement and why can we win? 3. Where is our movement today and how can it lead to victory?

1. What is today's globalization & what does it mean?
Today's globalization is globalization in the electronic age. It brings together high technology, global capital, the dominant power of global corporations, and neoliberal policies. Together these forces create maximum profit for global corporations through their unrestricted access to all markets - finance, goods and services, and labor around the world.

High technology (e.g., electronics, computers, information technology, and automation) has revolutionized the tools and technologies of production, transportation, communication and domination. Goods and services are produced and distributed with less and less human labor more and more quickly, and knowledge itself is an increasingly valuable commodity. The technologies of domination are more and more powerful and deadly.

Global capital, employing these new technologies, has restructured production, distribution and power relations. The historic driving force of capital - maximizing profit - now takes place in increasingly global markets for labor and goods and services, for finance and communication. Capital flows electronically and instantaneously around the globe 24 hours a day. Goods and services are sold in markets around the globe 24 hours a day. And people communicate in cyberspace around the globe 24 hours a day.

The dominant power of global corporations now rules the world through international institutions such as the International Monetary Fund (IMF), World Bank (WB), and World Trade Organization (WTO), etc. Global corporations' need to maximize profit in the new global economy is the driving force for today's neoliberal policies in developing as well as developed countries around the world. The race to the bottom is on, the social contract is gone, oppression is on the rise, and the rich are richer than they have ever been.

2. Why do we need a global movement & why can we win?

Armed with this understanding of today's globalization, we can say with confidence that we need a global movement. The economic and political forces we are fighting are global - the global corporations, international institutions, and neoliberal policies. Nation states and, of course, local and state governments, are losing power to global corporations and international institutions. And, from our bottom-up perspective, we must create a global vision and global strategy that can only emerge from a global movement.

Global corporations, with all of their wealth, are totally immoral. Scarcity is alive and growing in a world that is technologically capable of killing it off. Today's high technology has created a world of abundance. There is no objective reason for hunger, homelessness, lack of health care and education, environmental destruction, etc., except for the greed and power of global corporations and their drive for maximum profit.

We can win because we have the technology and abundance to provide a wonderful life for all the world's 6+ billion people, not just the rich and super rich. The future hangs in the leadership and strategic direction of our movement.

3. Where is our movement today & how can it lead to victory?

Today the global movement for economic and social justice is at the beginning stage of coalescing. We all know about the thousands who demonstrated in Seattle in 1999 and in Washington, DC in 2000 against globalization and neoliberalism. But fewer know about the thousands who demonstrated in Columbia, SC against the Confederate flag flying over the state capitol and in Tallahassee, FL against Jeb Bush's policy to end affirmative action.

Clearly, the movement is gathering momentum. Every year since 2001 thousands of activists and movement builders from across the globe have gathered in January at the World Social Forum under the slogan "Another World is Possible." Our global justice and equality movement is drawing in more and more people, and getting closer to a leap in activity and intensity. This leap will mean a new quality in the movement - a critical mass of people who are conscious of the global and systemic root causes of our problems and who are engaged in the struggles to fundamentally transform our world.

We are in the leadership development phase in the movement building process. How we prepare for the upsurge when millions enter the fight will, in large measure, determine which direction it will go - ours or theirs.

What this means for conscious moveme building folk is that we must focus on developing a bottom-up leadership that is broad and deep. It must include leaders from all sections of society but concentrate on those most adversely affected. This phase of leadership development requires a process of education, with popular education being an important tool to create a shared vision and winning strategy. This is essential if we are to be ready for the leap in our movement - to ensure that it does not compromise and to secure and hold onto victory. Our movement depends on people who are ready - who come to the truth of the moment and are prepared to engage.

Make it happen!

April 2005

Glossary of Key Terms

MAI (Multilateral Agreement on Investment) - A low profile global investment scheme designed to further limit government regulations and would give sweeping authority to corporations over government interests. Grassroots and citizen groups successfully defeated MAI from being agreed upon in the OEDC or WTO.

Bottom-Up Globalization - International economic development based on grassroots participation, democracy, and social justice. It is the alternative to Corporate (or Top Down) Globalization.

Climate Change - The increase in global surface temperature of the Earth, which is believed to negatively affect our ecosystem. Many argue that climate change, or the greenhouse effect, is the result of unregulated big business releasing chemicals into the atmosphere.

Central American Free Trade Agreement (CAFTA) - A preferential trading agreement being negotiated among Central American nations and the United States. It is modeled after NAFTA, which has been a disaster for small farmers and working people in Canada, the United States, and Mexico. Many feel CAFTA would be a solid step towards FTAA-style agreements.

COINTELPRO - COunter INTELligence PROgram of the FBI. COINTELPROs are the FBI domestic counter-intelligence programs developed to destroy individuals and organizations considered to be politically objectionable by the FBI. Targets of COINTELPRO have included the Black Power Movement, especially the Black Panther Party (BPP), the Civil Rights movement, American Indian Movement (AIM), Puerto Rican independence groups, and Central American solidarity groups.

Cold War - After WWII, the relationship between the United States and Soviet Union. There was political tension based on a military arms race. The US government feared new movements and emerging nation-states would align with the USSR and led many covert operations to destroy democratic and liberation movements throughout Africa and Latin America.

Colonialism - A power relationship in which an external nation state (colonizer) directly controls the political and economic system of another nation state and/or people (colony). Involves the presence of a military force to crush dissent and the migration of people from the colony to the nation state of the colonizer.

Commodification - Turning basic goods and services into products for capitalist financial markets.

Protest against CAFTA in Costa Rica

Comprehensive Development Framework (CDF) - The "new" set of policies at the WB/IMF designed to replace Structural Adjustment Programs (SAPs). Officially the policies are to reduce poverty through more efficient use of resources. They are also supposed to improve economic development, stability, and sustainability. In reality, these policies are no different than SAPs.

Corporate Globalization - An aspect of capitalism which drives expansion of the economic market system across the globe in search of maximum profits. Globalization is more than 500 years-old and has run constant throughout the three major stages of the capitalist global economy.

Cultural Imperialism - Imposing a country's worldview, values and lifestyle on others. Many critics of today's globalization use this term to describe how the United States actively exports its ideology of consumerism and free-market capitalism.

Direct Aid/Material Aid - Providing support to people's struggles in other countries. This support can be either economic (through monetary or material donations) or political (pressuring home governments to either support the struggle or end support for the struggle's enemies), but it is not linked to a domestic fight.

Fast Track - Term used to describe authority given to the President of the US by Congress to sidestep the Constitution regarding treaty negotiation. Fast Track authority allows the President to negotiate a treaty (always related to expanding neoliberal policies) quickly by limiting Congress to a "yes" or "no" vote without amendment. Fast Track is now called "Trade Promotion Authority."

Fourth World - Nations forcefully incorporated into states which maintain a distinct political culture but are internationally unrecognized. It usually refers to indigenous people.

Free Trade Agreement of the Americas (FTAA) - An extension of NAFTA that would apply to the entire Western Hemisphere. Popular movements have actively opposed the FTAA and have blocked its intended adoption on January 1, 2005.

GATS - General Agreement on Trade in Services. A set of international rules incorporated into the WTO for the liberalization of more than 160 services including telecommunications, banking & investment, transport, education, health, and the environment.

GATT - General Agreement on Tariffs and Trade. Created in 1948 from the Bretton Woods conference, this treaty focuses on promoting world trade by pressuring countries to reduce tariffs. It has formed the foundation for today's global institutions like the WTO.

Globalization - Also known as Corporate Globalization or Top-Down Globalization. An aspect of capitalism which drives expansion of the economic market system across the globe in search of maximum profits. Globalization is more than 500 years old and has run constant throughout the three major stages of the capitalist global economy.

Global North - Refers to the wealthy and more technologically advanced industrialized countries. They are referred to by geography since most of these countries are in the Northern hemisphere, although not all are.

Global South - Refers to the developing countries also known as the "Third World." They are referred to by geography since most of these countries are in the Southern hemisphere, although not all are.

Global South Within Global North - Refers to areas of concentrated poverty and political repression within the "Global North."

Gross Domestic Product (GDP) - The total value of goods produced and services provided in a country in one year.

Gross National Product (GNP) - The gross domestic product plus the total of net income from abroad.

Heterosexism - A system of oppression that grants institutional and cultural privileges to anyone who conforms to "traditional" gender roles. It either penalizes or disregards the lives of lesbian, gay, bisexual, questioning, and transgender people as well as alternative family structures.

Homophobia - An irrational fear of sexual attraction to the same gender or sex. Also, a term for all aspects of the oppression of LGBTQ people.

IFIs - International Financial Institutions. This refers to all international institutions of globalization such as the World Bank and the IMF.

Congolese Women protest for peace

CE QUE LA FEMME VEUT, DIEU LE VEUT
LES MAMANS CONGOLAISES VEULENT LA PAIX

IMF - International Monetary Fund. Institution developed at the Bretton Woods conference in 1944that first began to implement neoliberal policies. First mandated to regulate an international monetary system to facilitate global trade while leaving sovereign governments in charge of their own financial policies, the IMF now lends to countries in economic crisis and requires severe changes in economic policy including reduced money supply, reduced government spending, privatization, and the removal of restriction on capital flow.

Imperialism - A stage of advanced capitalism in which more powerful and developed nation states dominate less powerful and less developed countries and territories through military force and indirect political control.

Imperialism provides economic gain through access to raw materials, cheap labor, and markets for goods & services, and it often serves strategic geopolitical purposes.

Keynesianism - A theory of modern capitalist economics which holds that full employment is not a natural condition of capitalism and requires government spending on public works and direct financial support to the unemployed to keep the economy healthy.

LGBTQ - Lesbian, Gay, Bisexual, Transgender and Questioning. Other terms include LesBiGayTrans or Queer.

NAFTA - North American Free Trade Agreement. A treaty between Canada, the USA, and Mexico which deregulates trade between the three (also referred to as a "ménage a trade"). Put into effect on January 1, 1994, NAFTA has lowered wages, resulted in job losses, and eroded environmental and safety standards in all 3 countries.

Nationalism - A sense of national consciousness exalting one nation above all others and placing primary emphasis on promotion of its economic & political interests and culture as opposed to those of other nations.

Neocolonialism - A power relationship in which an external nation state indirectly controls the political and economic system of another nation state and/or people – often former colonies. May involve the presence of a military force to crush dissent and the migration of people from the former colony to the colonizer.

Neoliberalism - The philosophy of corporate globalization. It is the dominant set of economic & political policies guiding this stage of capitalist globalization. Its main points include: total rule of the "free" market, reduced social spending particularly on safety nets for workers and the poor, deregulation, privatization, as well as increased political and military domination domestically and globally.

NGO - Non-Governmental Organization. Also referred to as non-profits.

Organization for Economic Cooperation and Development (OEDC) - Founded in 1961, this elite group of North American and European countries provides space to develop economic plans and policies

Pan-Africanism - An analysis developed in the early 20th century calling for a world union of African people in spite of differences in geographical location, religion, and culture.

Patriarchy - A system of power based on the supremacy and dominance of men through the exploitation and oppression of women. Also referred to as sexism.

Popular - Of the people. Indicates a mass base or accessibility to a mass of people (e.g., popular education).

Prison Industrial Complex (PIC) - Neoliberal policies, practices and institutions of all levels of government designed to remove the discarded (those who are unemployable, poor, uneducated, etc.) from society to further the social control of those negatively impacted by globalization.

Privatization - The transfer of government-owned or managed (i.e. public) services, agencies, or property to corporations.

Race to the Bottom - Phrase used by popular movements to describe deteriorating living & working conditions of the majority of the world's population under corporate globalization and neoliberalism. Attributes include automation, downsizing, falling wages, eroded environmental protections, contingent labor, welfare "reform" and elimination, and increased global competition among workers.

Ruling Interests - Members of society who own and control society's wealth and make decisions for the rest of the population; predominantly made up of heads of state and corporations.

SAPs - Structural Adjustment Programs. A set of neoliberal policies created in 1970s and 1980s and forced on poor countries by the IMF and World Bank. Countries facing an economic crisis are forced to accept a series of conditions as part of receiving international loans. The conditions (reduction of money supply, reduced government spending, privatization, and removal of restriction on the flow of capital) have exacerbated poverty, caused widespread environmental degradation, and transferred wealth from the developing countries in

Image by Eric Drooker: www.drooker.com

the South to the industrialized countries in the North. Although SAPs are widely considered a failure and have been officially abandoned the same principle and programs still operate at both the IMF and World Bank.

Social Contract - The understanding between government and the population that a social safety net (government policies for unemployment, social security, welfare, etc.) would be maintained.

Solidarity - *"International solidarity is not an act of charity. It is an act of unity between allies fighting on different terrains toward the same objective. The foremost of these objectives is to aid the development of humanity to the highest level possible."* - Samora Machel (1933-1986), Leader of FRELIMO, First President of Mozambique

State - The political organization of the members or representatives of the political and economic elite in a society -- including legislative, executive, judicial, and military bodies.

Uruguay Round - The GATT negotiation round, begun in 1986 and ended in 1995, which led to the creation of the World Trade Organization (WTO) and the expansion of GATT into areas such as services, intellectual property rights (IPRs), and finance & securities.

Washington Consensus - The theory that good economic performance requires reduced government spending, deregulation, free flow of capital, privatization, and property rights. It was coined after a meeting of conservative Latin American and Caribbean policy-makers, representatives of international agencies, and members of academic and "think-tank" communities to evaluate the progress following the debt crisis of the 1980s.

Wedge Issues - Use of stereotypes to divide oppressed groups and prevent a mass-based movement (e.g., promoting the belief that immigrants take jobs from African-Americans so African-Americans should support repressive immigration laws).

White Supremacy - A system of power based on the supremacy and dominance of "white" people. "White" is a political concept created by the European and colonial ruling elite of the 17th and 18th centuries.

World Bank - Institution created from the Bretton Woods conference. Originally the International Bank for Reconstruction and Development, it was established to help finance the reconstruction of Europe after World War II and the development of poorer countries.

WTO - World Trade Organization. Created in 1995 by provisions in the "Uruguay Round" of the GATT negotiations, the WTO is an international organization of more than 140 countries. It serves as a forum for negotiating international trade agreements and the monitoring and regulating body for enforcing agreements. By targeting "non-tariff barriers to trade" (like environmental, labor or safety laws), the WTO can overturn local and national laws in secret and without an appeals process.

What is Popular Education?

Project South: Institute for the Elimination of Poverty & Genocide

Definitions for Popular Education

popular education, n. **1.** [Education for liberation] — Popular education is essential in developing new leadership to build a bottom-up movement for fundamental social change, justice and equality; see also **liberation, revolution, social and economic equality.**

2. [Accessible and relevant] — We begin by telling our stories, sharing and describing our lives, experiences, problems, and how we feel about them.

3. [Interactive] — We learn by doing: we participate in dialogue and activities that are fun, including cultural arts such as drama, drawing, music, poetry, and video.

4. [Education with an attitude] — We are not neutral: through dialogue and reflection we are moved to act collectively — creating change that will solve the problems of those at the bottom in our communities, those of us who are most oppressed, exploited, and marginalized.

5. [Egalitarian] — We are equal. All of us have knowledge to share and teach. All of us are listeners and learners, creating new knowledge and relationships of trust as we build for our future.

6. [Historic] — We see our experience within the context of history, indicating where we have come from and where we are going.

7. [Inclusive] — We see ourselves in relation to all people, including those of different ethnic groups and nationalities, social classes, ages, genders, sexualities, and abilities.

8. [Consciousness raising] — We critically analyze our experiences, explaining the immediate causes of our problems and discovering the deeper root causes in the structures of the economy, political institutions, and culture.

9. [Visionary] — We are hopeful, creating an optimistic vision of the community and global society we want for ourselves and our families.

10. [Strategic] — We are moved to collective action, developing a plan for short-term actions to address the immediate causes of our problems, and long-term movement building to address the root causes of our problems.

11. [Involves the whole person] — We use our head for analysis, reflection and consciousness; our heart for feeling and vision; and our feet for collective action for the short term and the long haul.

Tips & Guidelines for Creating A Community of Learners

Popular education is about creating a community of learners — each person in the group is a teacher, a learner, and a member of the community created by the workshop.

The following *Facilitator/Participant Tips* are designed to help this community form on the basis of equality. While most of these suggestions may seem like common sense, it is always helpful for group members and facilitators alike to take a moment to review them before a workshop begins.

Project South Youth Council Facilitators

Being Accountable to the group process (facilitator/participant tips)

1) Keep the task of the group in mind at all times. Group Discussion is an effort to bring out wide variety of ideas and understanding. It is not a debate nor a clash of wills. It is a proces of clarifying the issues faced by all group members.

2) If the group strays too far, you as a facilitator or group participant should help bring the group back to the task at hand.

3) Be aware of time limitations. Watch the clock and remind the group if it seems behind schedule. Sometimes it is helpful to choose a timekeeper.

4) Keep track of who's participating in the group and who is not. Draw out the quiet member In an active group, you can offer that person an opening simply by asking what s/he thinks.

5) Be aware of your own participation. Share your best ideas. If you find it easy to talk, be brief and to the point. Change topics only when the whole group is ready for the change.

Project South Process for Guidelines in Group Discussion

Guidelines can be used as a tool for workshop facilitators and participants. The 4 Steps & Guidelines listed below are suggestions based on our experience in conducting Project South workshops.

1 Go over each point in the guidelines so everyone has the same understanding of what they mean. Ask if anyone would like to add additional points. If so, review the additions so all participants agree on what they mean.

2 Ask if anyone disagrees with a point and would like it removed. The group should reach consensus on removing a point.

3 Once everyone agrees on the guidelines, ask the participants whether or not they agree to these guidelines for the duration of the workshop.

4 Silence does not equal consent! Ask participants to say yes or no. If consensus cannot be reached, the group should decide whether or not to proceed with the workshop. (It is extremely rare for a group to disagree on the guidelines.)

Our Guidelines

Be Aware of Time

Use The "Whoa"

Respect the Strengths & Weaknesses of All

Step Up, Step Back

Oppression Exists: Not in our Space

Open Minds Only

Project South Guidelines: An Explanation

Be Aware of Time
There is time to explore points and ask questions. There is not time for speeches or storytelling that do not address the task at hand.

Use The "Whoa"
If at some point during the workshop a participant does not understand what has been said, strongly disagrees, or has something vital to share (like the room is on fire), they should raise their hand and say, "Whoa." This will focus attention on their question or point. Participants should exercise restraint when using the "Whoa." (See above, "Be Aware of Time.")

Respect the Strengths & Weaknesses of All
Youth, educators, grassroots activists, and scholars all have their respective areas of expertise. It's important that during a workshop, everyone can learn from one another as well as bring their experience into the community.

Step Up, Step Back
Participants who like to talk should "step back" and create a space for those who are quiet. Quiet people should "step up" and contribute to the group so that all may learn. All participants have an equal opportunity to participate during workshops and small group sessions. Facilitators will help draw out quieter people and ensure that more vocal people do not dominate.

Oppression Exists But not in our Space
The existence of oppression (racism, classism, sexism, homophobia /heterosexism, etc.) is not debatable. Oppressive behavior will not be tolerated. This means that the workshop space will be a space where oppression is actively confronted.

Open Minds Only
Participants should leave their agendas and dogma at the door when they are in a group discussion.

Lessons Learned from History

Project South: Institute for the Elimination of Poverty & Genocide

History & Popular Education:
Critically Remembering Our Past

Cesar Chavez: United Farm Workers Union

In order to figure out where we are going, and how to get there - it helps to understand where we have come from. History can help us understand how the social and economic conditions we face today were created and developed. History teaches us that the positive things we enjoy today were won by the collective struggles of groups of 'ordinary' folks in the past.

Critically remembering our history through group discussions and activities can be an effective tool for movement building. This critical history is often substituted with a nostalgic version in our schools and textbooks. For example, most Americans remember the story of Rosa Parks and the Montgomery Bus Boycott. However the memory that most people have is of a lone, tired woman coming home from work who refused to give up her seat. This story would lead one to believe the Montgomery Bus Boycott was the spontaneous result of one woman's courage.

However, the real story includes the fact that Rosa Parks was active in the Montgomery NAACP and had received extensive training on non-violent direct action training from Ella Baker and Septima Clark at the Highlander Center in Tennessee. It also includes the fact that Rosa Parks was not the first to refuse her seat for political reasons and that the Montgomery Bus Boycott itself was the result of countless hours in planning and hard work by most of Black Montgomery and, particularly, the collective struggle of Montgomery's Black Women.

These two versions of the same history lead to very different conclusions and very different lessons learned for people struggling against oppression today.

Project South looks at history in a way that integrates economics, public policy, and popular movements. We explain that our education system encourages students to "focus" on a particular area but teaches us very little about how these pieces intersect to create the *Big Picture*. We have found that once communities and groups connect their struggle to the big picture, they feel less isolated and more aware of how to affect positive change in their communities.

Project South Timeline: Telling Our Story

The Project South timeline is our own unique version of a very old teaching method – storytelling. When the timeline is used as an introduction, we refer to it as an "Aha" Moment exercise. We ask participants to write down the moment when they first felt a part of a movement and place this on the timeline in its proper place.

Our Movement Building Timeline (shown below) presents significant events of the past 100 years in a three-line format. Each line represents a different force in society: major economic shifts and events, government programs and policies, and people's movements. Although we often think about these as three distinct categories, it's when we look at them together it becomes clear that each force impacts the other.

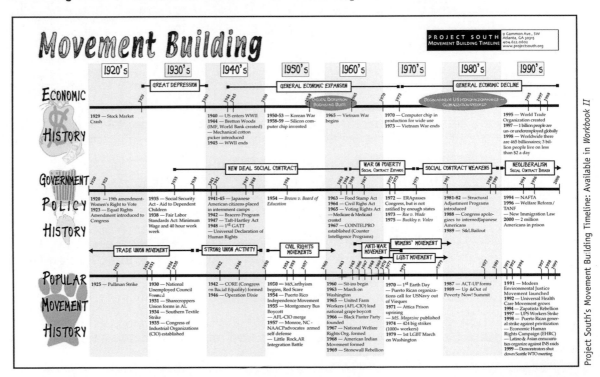

Talking about the Timeline: In schools and in life we are often taught very little about how the Economy works and its relationship to Government Policy. At Project South, we say, *Economic History* is about what happens with money and markets, *Government Policy* are laws and procedures determined by our elected officials - in Congress, the state house or city hall, and *Popular* (of the people) *Movements* are the history of our struggles and achievements. If we are taught anything about these movements it is usually about one leader or one event. And we are rarely taught that movements impact public policy, or are related to the economy.

Project South: Institute for the Elimination of Poverty & Genocide

Project South Presents: *Today's Globalization Time*

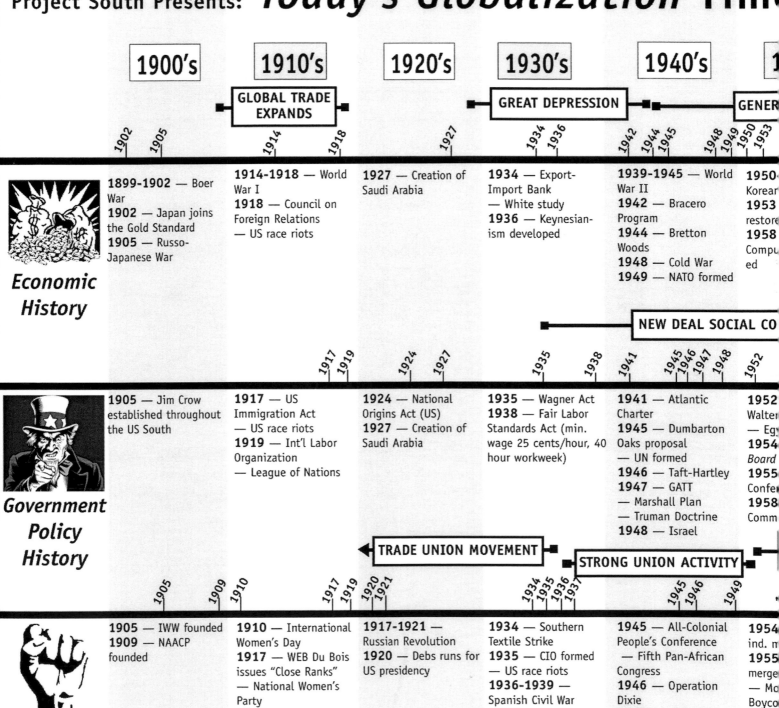

	1900's	1910's	1920's	1930's	1940's	1
		GLOBAL TRADE EXPANDS		**GREAT DEPRESSION**	**GENER**	

Economic History

1902	1905	1914	1918	1927	1934	1936	1942	1944	1945	1948	1949	1950	1953

1899-1902 — Boer War
1902 — Japan joins the Gold Standard
1905 — Russo-Japanese War

1914-1918 — World War I
1918 — Council on Foreign Relations — US race riots

1927 — Creation of Saudi Arabia

1934 — Export-Import Bank — White study
1936 — Keynesian-ism developed

1939-1945 — World War II
1942 — Bracero Program
1944 — Bretton Woods
1948 — Cold War
1949 — NATO formed

1950 Korean
1953 restore
1958 Compu ed

NEW DEAL SOCIAL CO

Government Policy History

1917	1919	1924	1927	1935	1938	1941	1945	1946	1947	1948	1952

1905 — Jim Crow established throughout the US South

1917 — US Immigration Act — US race riots
1919 — Int'l Labor Organization — League of Nations

1924 — National Origins Act (US)
1927 — Creation of Saudi Arabia

1935 — Wagner Act
1938 — Fair Labor Standards Act (min. wage 25 cents/hour, 40 hour workweek)

1941 — Atlantic Charter
1945 — Dumbarton Oaks proposal — UN formed
1946 — Taft-Hartley
1947 — GATT — Marshall Plan — Truman Doctrine
1948 — Israel

1952 Walter — Egy
1954 *Board*
1955 Confe
1958 Comm

◄ TRADE UNION MOVEMENT   **STRONG UNION ACTIVITY**

Popular Movement History

1905	1909	1910	1917	1919	1920	1921	1934	1935	1936	1937	1945	1946	1949

1905 — IWW founded
1909 — NAACP founded

1910 — International Women's Day
1917 — WEB Du Bois issues "Close Ranks" — National Women's Party
1919 — Seattle General Strike — Sleeping Car Porters organized

1917-1921 — Russian Revolution
1920 — Debs runs for US presidency

1934 — Southern Textile Strike
1935 — CIO formed — US race riots
1936-1939 — Spanish Civil War
1937 — Abraham Lincoln Brigades

1945 — All-Colonial People's Conference — Fifth Pan-African Congress
1946 — Operation Dixie
1949 — Chinese Revolution

1954 ind. m
1955 merge — Ma Boyco
1956 Africa
1959 Revol
1959 Ameri

**Project South
Today's Globalization
Timeline**

**9 Gammon Avenue, SW
Atlanta, GA 30315
www.projectsouth.org**

eline

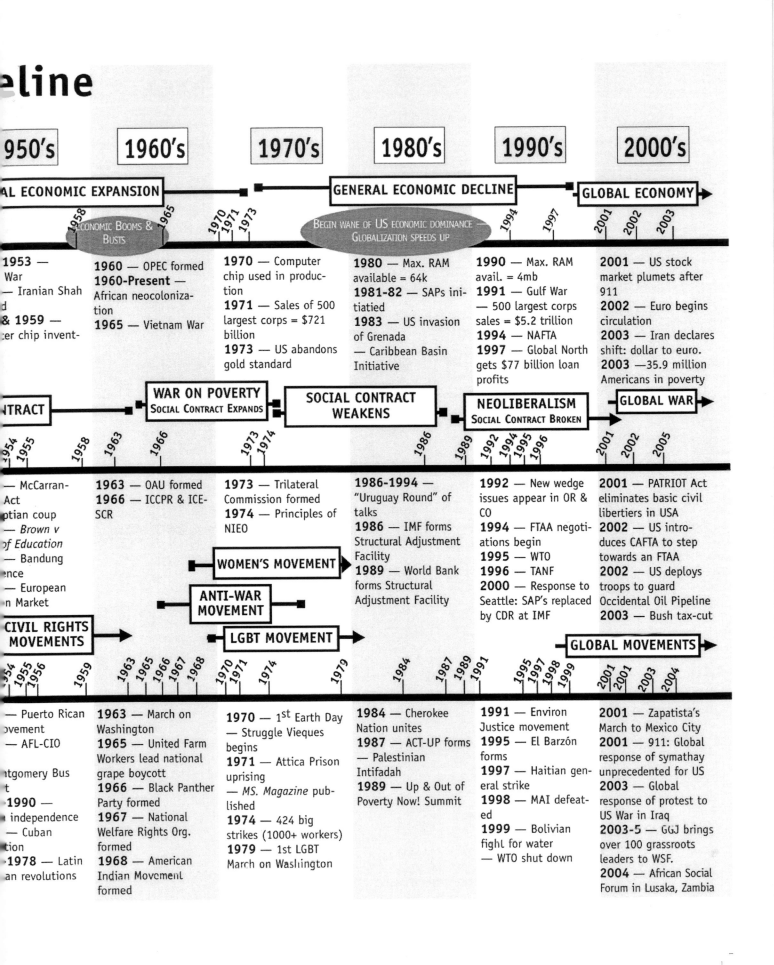

| 950's | 1960's | 1970's | 1980's | 1990's | 2000's |

AL ECONOMIC EXPANSION → **GENERAL ECONOMIC DECLINE** → **GLOBAL ECONOMY** →

1958 *1965* *1970 1971 1973* *1994 1997* *2001 2002 2003*

ECONOMIC BOOMS & BUSTS

BEGIN WANE OF US ECONOMIC DOMINANCE — GLOBALIZATION SPEEDS UP

1953 —
War
— Iranian Shah
d
& **1959 —**
er chip invent-

1960 — OPEC formed
1960-Present — African neocoloniza-tion
1965 — Vietnam War

1970 — Computer chip used in produc-tion
1971 — Sales of 500 largest corps = $721 billion
1973 — US abandons gold standard

1980 — Max. RAM available = 64k
1981-82 — SAPs ini-tiated
1983 — US invasion of Grenada
— Caribbean Basin Initiative

1990 — Max. RAM avail. = 4mb
1991 — Gulf War
— 500 largest corps sales = $5.2 trillion
1994 — NAFTA
1997 — Global North gets $77 billion loan profits

2001 — US stock market plumets after 911
2002 — Euro begins circulation
2003 — Iran declares shift: dollar to euro.
2003 —35.9 million Americans in poverty

NTRACT → **WAR ON POVERTY** SOCIAL CONTRACT EXPANDS → **SOCIAL CONTRACT WEAKENS** → **NEOLIBERALISM** SOCIAL CONTRACT BROKEN → **GLOBAL WAR** →

1954 1955 *1958 1963 1966* *1973 1974* *1986 1989 1992 1994 1995 1996* *2001 2002 2005*

— McCarran-
Act
ptian coup
— *Brown v of Education*
— Bandung
ence
— European
n Market

1963 — OAU formed
1966 — ICCPR & ICE-SCR

1973 — Trilateral Commission formed
1974 — Principles of NIEO

1986-1994 —
"Uruguay Round" of talks
1986 — IMF forms Structural Adjustment Facility
1989 — World Bank forms Structural Adjustment Facility

1992 — New wedge issues appear in OR & CO
1994 — FTAA negoti-ations begin
1995 — WTO
1996 — TANF
2000 — Response to Seattle: SAP's replaced by CDR at IMF

2001 — PATRIOT Act eliminates basic civil libertiers in USA
2002 — US intro-duces CAFTA to step towards an FTAA
2002 — US deploys troops to guard Occidental Oil Pipeline
2003 — Bush tax-cut

WOMEN'S MOVEMENT →

ANTI-WAR MOVEMENT →

CIVIL RIGHTS MOVEMENTS →

LGBT MOVEMENT →

GLOBAL MOVEMENTS →

1954 1955 1956 1959 *1963 1965 1966 1967 1968* *1970 1971 1974 1979* *1984 1987 1989 1991* *1995 1997 1998 1999* *2001 2001 2003 2004*

— Puerto Rican
ovement
— AFL-CIO
ntgomery Bus
t
1990 —
independence
— Cuban
tion
1978 — Latin
an revolutions

1963 — March on Washington
1965 — United Farm Workers lead national grape boycott
1966 — Black Panther Party formed
1967 — National Welfare Rights Org. formed
1968 — American Indian Movement formed

1970 — 1st Earth Day
— Struggle Vieques begins
1971 — Attica Prison uprising
— *MS. Magazine* pub-lished
1974 — 424 big strikes (1000+ workers)
1979 — 1st LGBT March on Washington

1984 — Cherokee Nation unites
1987 — ACT-UP forms
— Palestinian Intifadah
1989 — Up & Out of Poverty Now! Summit

1991 — Environ Justice movement
1995 — El Barzón forms
1997 — Haitian gen-eral strike
1998 — MAI defeat-ed
1999 — Bolivian fight for water
— WTO shut down

2001 — Zapatista's March to Mexico City
2001 — 911: Global response of symathay unprecedented for US
2003 — Global response of protest to US War in Iraq
2003-5 — GGJ brings over 100 grassroots leaders to WSF.
2004 — African Social Forum in Lusaka, Zambia

A Bullet Point History of Globalization

Stages of Capitalist Development. The 3 stages are: **Mercantile**: widespread agriculture and colonialism with only an early manufacturing and professional class; **Industrial/Financial**: characterized by widespread use of machines in production, national markets within global production, global imperialism, and division of labor; **Electronic**: the latest period of capitalist globalization which uses computers, robotics & other electronic technology in production. This period (from the 1970s to present) has seen a breaking of the social contract and welfare state. Mechanized/robotic production replaces low skilled workers, and global financial institutions as the main tool of neo-colonialism and neoliberalism.

1482 · Portugal builds Elmina Castle in Ghana, West Africa. The fort becomes the largest slave trading post in the world where enslaved Africans are held before being sent across the Atlantic.[1]

1492-Present · The European Conquest of the Americas. Genocide of the indigenous peoples of the Americas begins with Columbus landing on Hispanola. The population of indigenous people in the hemisphere drops from 80-100 million at Columbus' landing to 10 million by the 1600s.

1497 · First Portuguese voyage to and from India around South Africa. The desire for new trading markets launches colonial conquest.

1526 · Pee Dee River community of South Carolina. Slave rebellion against the Spanish unites enslaved Africans with Native Americans. The "Black Indians" of the Pee Dee River set up the first colony on the continent that practices equality of all people.

1650 · Bolivian Silver Mines. Using a system of slavery called *mita*, Spain extracts silver from Bolivia to finance the conquest of new land in the Americas. The system is based on Indian slave labor. Between 1492 and 1650, almost 8 million indigenous people die in the Potosí mines alone.[2]

1652 · The Dutch settle at the Cape of Good Hope on the southern tip of Africa. Controlling the Cape means controlling the access to the Indian Ocean and markets there.[3]

1672-1864 · Maroon Communities. Numbering roughly 50 communities in eight southern US states, these communities of runaway slaves and Native Americans provide safe havens and launch raids to free slaves. One of the most famous of these raids was lead by Mingoe in 1691.

1717 · Britain establishes the gold standard. Sir Isaac Newton, as Master of the Mint, helps England define its currency to gold. This means the value of the British currency (the pound) is fixed to a certain amount of gold.[4]

1758 · The first American Indian reservation is established. This strategy for conquering land and containing people will be copied in later ages by South Africa and Israel.

1770 · Great Bengal Famine. Although South Asia had known famine before the British invasion, local response had addressed the problem. The famine under British rule resulted in more then 10 million dead or about 1/3 of the total population. The high death rate is attributed to the East India Company's and colonial authority's practice of isolating limited relief and continuing to export food to Britain during the famine. Bengal would go on to suffer 6 more famines where millions would needlessly die from starvation. This demonstrates one of the purposes of a colony- to provide raw materials (in this case food) regardless of the effect on the local populace.[5]

1776 · United States Revolution. This first successful anti-colonial revolution signaled the beginning of the end for the first world colonial order. France's involvement as an ally of the United States during the war helped deepen an economic crisis within the French government. The resulting financial crisis contributes to the French Revolution, and the rise of Napoleon. Napoleon's forced abdication of the Spanish throne throws Spanish America into a crisis of legitimate government. A new form of colonialism arises which emphasizes the colonies as possible markets and is favored by the British economic elite who profit on the relative weakness of France and Spain. The result is devastating on local industry in many parts of the world as European goods flood the markets using a mixture of market forces and military might.[6]

· **English economist Adam Smith publishes <u>The Wealth of Nations</u>.** The first treatise on economic liberalism, the book calls for total unrestricted free trade with the government completely hands off on all economic matters. The theories remain prevalent until the Great Depression of the 1930s. They surface again in the 1970s.[7]

1779 · Slavery in the US. There are 750,000 slaves in the United States, mostly in the South. By 1860 there are 4.4 million African Americans, 90% in the South and almost 90% are slaves. In total, about 50 million Africans are forcibly taken from Africa, 10-15 million survive the middle passage to be enslaved throughout the Americas.

1780 · The first war between the Bantu tribe and the Boer (Dutch) settlers in South Africa occurs.[8]

1793 · Fugitive Slave Act. Although laws already exist which returned escaped slaves to their owners, the US Congress passes the Fugitive Slave Act. This law allows owners to recover slaves merely by presenting proof of ownership before a magistrate. Escaped slaves are forbidden a jury trial or the right to give evidence. After the law is passed free Blacks in the North are sometimes kidnapped and taken south.

1794-1803 · Haitian Revolution. Building on the "Declaration on the Rights of Man," France abolishes slavery in its colonies. However, French planters in St. Domingue refuse the Black population citizenship. The enslaved Africans on the island begin a guerrilla campaign for freedom and are eventually joined by the "free" people of color. In 13 years of simultaneous wars and revolutions with Spain, France, white planters, white settlers, enslaved Blacks and free mulattos, the people of Haiti eventually prevail and form the first independent Black country in the Western hemisphere. More importantly, Haiti is the first successful slave revolt under the modern institution of slavery. As the threat of a good example, it is immediately targeted by the US and other colonial powers for destabilization.[9]

1795 · The Dutch end the slave trade in Africa.[10]

1808 · Great Britain and the US agree to end the transatlantic slave trade.[11] For the US, this simultaneously limits the numbers of Blacks (seen as a constant threat to whites) in the country and limits the expansion of southern agricultural capital.

1817 · Ricardo develops theory of "comparative advantage." In <u>Principles of Political Economy, and Taxation</u> British economist David Ricardo develops the theory that countries should find their market niche by specializing their production of goods to those in which they have a natural advantage (for example, Cuba producing sugar). He believes this would benefit both buyers and sellers. Although this theory is still the basis for much of the current discussion of globalization, the two conditions Ricardo insists must be present - balanced trade between countries regarded as equals and local investment capital which is restricted from flowing out of high-wage countries to low-wage countries - are not present in today's globalization. Instead, countries are encouraged to survive through exports while being subservient to foreign capital.[12]

1821 · Liberia is formed by ex-slaves from the US. The American Colonization Society is appointed custodian of "recaptives" under its protection. Although many whites see freed Blacks as a way of promoting Christianity in Africa, others see free Blacks in the US as a threat. By 1870, 13,000 immigrants are settled in Liberia. 60% are emancipated slaves.[13]

1823 · Monroe Doctrine. After England loses the war of 1812, it realizes that gaining additional colonies in the Western hemisphere would be too costly. President Monroe declares that any European intervention in the Americas would be considered unfriendly to the US. This is in line with British interests. Great Britain, with the most powerful navy in the world, helps the US enforce this policy. Any European powers operating in the Western hemisphere would find themselves in a conflict with the US which would have the British as an ally. This doctrine allowed the US to extend its dominance throughout Latin America while also restricting the colonial holdings of European powers.[14]

1825 · Latin American Independence from Spain. The indigenous people of the Western hemisphere had always resisted European invasion. From the guerrilla warfare of the Taino and Caribe in the Caribbean to the revolts in the Peruvian Andes and pueblos of New Mexico, native people had resisted the conquest with mixed success. By the 19th century, however, resistance to imperialism had become the cause of the aristocracy. Predominantly of European ancestry, these individuals (like Juan Manuel de Rosas in Argentina and Gabriel García Moreno in Ecuador and Porfio Diaz in Mexico) were usually large landowners who used their wealth to wage a war for independence from Spain. This was not done in the name of any specific ideology but to secure wealth and power. The struggles against Spain in Latin America did not question the existing economic structure, only the political one. Even then the struggle was about who should be in control of exploiting local resources, the wealthy of Spain or the wealthy of the colonies.

1830 · The Indian Removal Act. Congress gives President Andrew Jackson the legal tool to relocate all Native Americans to Indian Territory west of the Mississippi. The second Seminole War is fought against this aggression. The Seminoles (means *runaway* in Creek) fight the US Army costing the government $40 million and 1500 troops. The Seminoles too are finally defeated and forced with five other tribes into the Trail of Tears.

1834 · Slavery abolished in Great Britain.[15]

1846 · Great Britain repeals the Corn Laws which heavily tax-imported grain. This begins the world tendency to reduce trade barriers.[16]

1846-1848 · Mexican-American War. After white settlers immigrate to Texas, rebel, and then are annexed by the US, the ruling class continues to lust for California. Polk order troops to the Rio Grande river and these troops are interpreted by Mexico to be a show of force. The US forces are attacked by Mexico, and war follows. Mexico is badly defeated and loses about half of its territory including what is now Utah, Nevada, California, and most of Arizona for a paltry $15 million payment. Although the Treaty of Guadalupe-Hidalgo supposedly gives rights to those Mexicans living in what is now the US, the document is not taken seriously.[17]

1853 · US invades Japan with Gunboat Diplomacy. Under the order of President Millard Filmore to open relations with Japan, Commodore Perry steams into Tokyo harbor. He tells the Tokugawa Shogunate (the ruling military family) to change their policy of isolation or the fleet will burn Tokyo. The Shogunate complies. The US is now regularly using its military to open foreign markets.[18]

1857 · The Great Rebellion in Northern India. After years of torture, cultural genocide, and forcing Western ideas upon India, particularly the soldiers, the British strategy of divide & conquer backfires. The new Lee-Enfield .303 rifle is issued to soldiers. This weapon requires the soldier to bite the end of the cartridge which is covered in pig fat or beef tallow. When Hindu and Muslim soldiers of the 3rd regiment (light cavalry) are given the new Enfield rifle and ordered to fire, they refuse for religious reasons. This is the last straw in a long line of indignities. They are imprisoned, but the 11th and 20th cavalry turn on their officers. This ignites a peasant uprising in the country which lasts over a year and is eventually defeated by the British. However, it begins a chain of resistance which leads to Indian independence after World War II.[19]

1858 · The British Parliament takes control of India away from the British East India Company.[20]

1859 · Harper's Ferry - Harriet Tubman, founder of the Underground Railroad, recruits for the Harper's Ferry struggle. John Brown and 22 others attempt to secure arms for a massive slave revolt. Though it fails, Harper's Ferry further polarizes the country and brings the Civil War closer.

1861-1865 · The US Civil War. After almost a century of building tension, industrial capital in the North and agrarian capital in the South go to war. 600,000 die on both sides. 200,000 Blacks are in the army and navy, and 38,000 are killed. The free labor of enslaved Africans is seen as a threat to northern industrialism. The issue splits the political & economic elite into North and South, and both sides use force to protect their interests. By prohibiting Southern plantations from profiting off slavery, Northern industrialists ensure their financial success and are fully able to turn their attention to the rest of the hemisphere.

1866-1891 · US Genocide of Native People

Continues. The US military, having won the Civil War, focuses its attention on the ongoing physical extermination and spiritual genocide of Native Americans, and continues the policy of concentrating all remaining Indians in the West onto reservations. The US violates treaty agreements with the Lakota councils and forces the nation to defend their land. On June 25, 1876, Crazy Horse leads Lakota and Cheyenne warriors in the stinging defeat of Custer and his men at Little Big Horn; and with Red Cloud, also of the Oglala Lakota, delivers yet another great defeat to the US Army. In the closing decade of the 19th century, the US 7th Cavalry assassinates Hunkpapa Lakota chief Sitting Bull. Following this, chief Red Cloud invites Miniconjou chief Spotted Elk to Pine Ridge. Spotted Elk and 350 followers camp near Wounded Knee Creek where the 7th Cavalry massacres 300 mostly Miniconjou, including Spotted Elk, on December 28, 1890.

1867 · Reconstruction Act - Allows for the election of Black men, and as a result 2 senators and 20 Black congressman are elected from the South. Free public and integrated education is established. Black and White masses benefit from Reconstruction in terms of education, tax relief, access to credit, freedom of movement, and employment opportunities. The growing unity between ex-slaves and landless whites alarms the ruling interest who quickly move to crush it.

1870 · The Naturalization Act of 1870. This law prevents immigrants of China from gaining US citizenship, as well as prohibits the wives of Chinese laborers from coming to the US. The exploitation of immigrant labor for domestic development remains a part of US policy.[21]

1871 · Germany joins Great Britain in adopting the gold standard.[22]

· Earlier Age of Globalization. With the coming of the Industrial Revolution, intercontinental travel becomes easier. The cost of doing business around the world falls. Europe opens itself to overseas trade, lowering tariffs, and easing regulations. This sparks a level of international commerce not seen until later in the 20th century. Twenty percent (20%) of the collective Gross Domestic Product (GDP) of the world is in foreign assets. This will not happen again until 1985. Legal restrictions on travel are also eased, and 1/7 of the world working-age

population moves from one country to another from 1870 - 1925.[23]

1873 · Zanzibar closes its slave market. Established between 1811 and 1820, the slave market at Zanzibar catered primarily to the French and the Portuguese. Great Britain uses opposition to the slave trade to further its colonial holdings in Africa. Through a series of treaties with European powers and African sultans, the British succeed in restricting the trade and extending their range of influence. In 1873 the Sultan Barghash signs a treaty which ends the slave trade throughout his domain. The market is closed.[24]

· US changes to the gold standard.[25]

1877 · Hayes-Tilden Compromise. Republican Rutherford B. Hayes is declared president of the US on condition that Federal troops be withdrawn from the South. This is a major step in the dismantling of Reconstruction and opens the door for Black Codes and Jim Crow Constitutions. These laws & practices discourage unity among poor whites and people of color.

1882 · Chinese Exclusion Act. Congress bars Chinese workers from entering the US for 10 years. However, the law does not apply to merchants.[26]

1884 · The Berlin Conference. At the suggestion of Portugal, an international conference is held to settle territorial disputes in Africa. By establishing rules for occupying and colonizing the land and people, Africa is divided without a war among European countries. The arbitrary boundaries intentionally imposed on the continent divide similar ethnic groups and also force rival tribes into the same territory. These boundaries exist today.[27]

1885 · Indian National Congress is formed in India.[28]

1890 · British Imperialism in Southern Africa. After a visiting an unemployment rally in England, Cecil Rhodes becomes convinced of the use of foreign colonies as a way of reducing class tension in England. By trickery and warfare he gains control over the rich diamond fields of southern Africa, and in 1890 he is the prime minister and virtual dictator of the Cape Colony, encompassing most of the area. During his reign he institutes polices which guarantee political and economic power for whites only. The policies are copied in other parts of colonial Africa & remain despite the changes in political control.[29]

1893-1894 · Queen Liliuokalani of Hawaii is dethroned by US Marines. The US destroys the kingdom and annexes more than 2 million acres of land. Queen Liliuokalani calls on her people to organize, "There is still time to save our heritage. Never cease to act because you fear you may fail. The voice of the people is the voice of God."

1898 · Spanish American War. After the explosion of the U.S.S. Maine near Cuba, newspaper mogul William Randolph Hearst begins a misinformation campaign. The US declares war on Spain and invades Cuba and Puerto Rico, and later, the Philippines. Puerto Rico is kept as a direct colony and the Philippine Islands become a protectorate.

1899-1902 · Boer War Solidifies British Control of Southern Africa. Since the early 1800s the British had contested Dutch colonies in southern Africa. In 1814, Britain took over the Dutch colony at the Cape of Good Hope (called the "Cape Colony"). This insured British control of the passage to the Indian Ocean and the lucrative trading opportunities there. For the next 80 years, however, Dutch colonists (known as Boers) were pushed further and further North by the British. This reached a critical point when, at almost the same time, the Boer territory (the Transvaal republic) began industrialization and other European powers began staking claims to parts of Africa. With the possibility that English control of the Cape would be challenged by both the Transvaal achieving economic independence and military threats from other imperial powers, Great Britain moves to consolidate its holding in southern Africa. Britain's naval might ensured victory. The treaty in 1902 ends the Boer republic, but what was lost militarily by the Boers is gained politically. Within 10 years of the treaty, South Africa is formed and discrimination against Blacks and Asian immigrants is legislatively institutionalized.[30]

1902 · Japan joins in the Gold Standard. As Japan moves from an isolationist country to a colonial power, it adopts the prevailing European economic theory of the time and joins the Gold Standard. Japan suspends it during World War I and does not return to it until 1930. However, the next year Japan leaves the Gold Standard and introduces a policy similar to Keynesianism.

1905 · Russo-Japanese War. After a rapid change from isolationism, the Japanese government is eager to become a colonial power. The Russian Czar is eager for a short, victorious war to solidify public support. Both countries use disputes over Manchuria as a means of getting what they want. However, Japan wins decisively.[31]

· Industrial Workers of the World founded in Chicago. Mary Harris "Mother" Jones, "Big" Bill Haywood, Daniel DeLeon, and others participate in the founding convention of a revolutionary union. The IWW, also known as the Wobblies, adopt the strategy of industrial unionism where all workers in an industry are organized into one union. This is in stark contrast to the American Federation of Labor which organizes only those workers in professional crafts. The Wobblies organize unskilled workers, women, immigrants, & people of color. Its strategies of direct action & industrial militancy are eventually adopted by the CIO.

1909 · National Association for the Advancement of Colored People (NAACP) forms with central involvement from W.E.B. Du Bois, Mary White Ovington, and William English Walling. The mission is to address the large number of lynchings.

· Japanese plantation workers in Hawaii strike again for higher wages and better working conditions. On the island of Oahu, 7,000 strike the major plantations for four months.

1910 · International Women's Day (March 8) established. During the 1909 shirtwaist makers' strike—the largest strike of women in the United States to that time— hundreds of young women garment workers hit the streets to sell copies of a special edition of the New York *Call*, the city's Socialist newspaper. The Socialist Party had donated the paper free of charge to the strikers to help them raise money for the strike fund.

1910-1920 · Mexican Revolution. Oil imperatives led US to send troops to established present day boarder and squash anti-imperialist revolt.

1914-1918 · World War I. In a combination of 19th century colonialism and 20th century weaponry, the countries of Europe wage a four-year war which leaves 10 million dead and 20 million wounded. The Allied powers (Great Britain, France, Russia, Japan, Serbia, Italy, Portugal, Romania, the US, and Greece) go to war against the Central powers (Germany, Austria-Hungary, the Ottoman Empire, and Bulgaria) to determine, quite literally, who would control the world. At stake is the dominance of Europe and therefore present and future colonial holdings in the Middle East, Africa, and Asia. The use of modern weaponry (like the machine gun, airplane, early submarines, tanks, etc.) against 19th century strategies (like the infantry charge) leads to mass slaughter yet little change in territory. The Allied powers, particularly Britain, come out ahead with new colonial holdings in the Middle East, and therefore control of the oil supply. The great loss of life and economic hardship destroys the Austria-Hungary and Ottoman Empires, leads to an Arab revolt in Palestine, and a full-scale revolution in Russia.[32]

1917 · Immigration Act. Congress uses a set of geographic criteria to exclude Asian Indians from the US. The rationale is their racial and ethnic status is not clearly white or Black under the prevailing laws. The areas covered under the so-called Asiatic Barred Zone are countries of South and Southeast Asia as well as Pacific and Indian Ocean islands. The Act specifically does not cover Guam and the Philippines since these are newly acquired colonies.[33]

· Ku Klux Klan, in revival, sparks 26 riots across the country aimed at preventing Black voter registration and political participation.

· W.E.B. Du Bois issues a statement in *The Crisis* called "Close Ranks" to rally African American leaders in support of World War I efforts. Most leaders do support the war with the exception of A. Philip Randolph. More than 370,000 African-Americans are trained for combat. About 100,000 fight & perform with distinction.

· National Women's Party. Activists institute a direct action campaign in support of women's suffrage in the US, more than 200 women are arrested.

1917-1921 · Russian Revolution. After 3 years of war, the Russian economy is in shambles. A political revolution in 1905 had replaced the Tsar with a constitutionalist government (called the Provisional Government). By 1917 massive unrest among the people leads to the creation of peasant and workers' councils (soviets). In 1917 the soviets replace the Provisional Government as the base of power in the country. Counter-revolutionary forces organize an army (the White army) to bring back the Tsar. By 1921 they are defeated by the Red Army. The successful social revolution in Russia, which reorganizes the economy as well as political power, deeply frightens the capitalists of the West. Great Britain, France, Germany, the US, Japan and Canada each place troops in parts of the Russian empire in an attempt to counter the revolution or take advantage and grab territory.[34]

1918 · John Mayard Keynes Predicts Trouble in Europe. John Mayard Keynes represents Great Britain at the Supreme Economic Council which sets terms for German reparations after World War I. He eventually resigns in protest because the terms of the Versailles Treaty would keep Central Europe destabilized.[35]

· Council on Foreign Relations. Founded in 1918 as a "board of initiation," the organization is formed to foster cooperation among Western governments, international agencies, and corporations.

1919 · International Labor Organization. Established through the Treaty of Versailles, the ILO is founded to bring together employers, governments, and workers. It is one of the first international organizations ever to do so. The US joins in 1934.[36]

· League of Nations. After World War I, the League is formed to promote international peace and security. The basis of the League, the Covenant, is written into the Treaty of Versailles and other peace treaties and provides for an assembly, a council, and a secretariat. A system of colonial mandates is also set up. The US, which fails to ratify the Treaty of Versailles, never becomes a member. Based in Geneva, the League proves useful in settling minor international disputes, but is unable to stop aggression by major powers-e.g., Japan's occupation of Manchuria (1931), Italy's conquest of Ethiopia (1935-36), and Germany's seizure of Austria (1938). It collapses early in World War II and dissolves itself in 1946. The League establishes the first pattern of permanent international organization and serves as a model for its successor, the United Nations.

· **Seattle General Strike.** After World War I ends, unions are no longer bound by the no-strike clause. Labor demands its due. With the success of the Russian Revolution, workers around the world are more militant, more willing to strike and are more confident of their power. 32,000 workers at the Seattle shipyards lead a strike which grows into a citywide general strike, the first in the US. The strike is so complete that the mayor must appear before the labor council to ask for certain services.

· **A. Philip Randolph serves as editor of the socialist monthly,** *The Messenger*, and organizes the Brotherhood of Sleeping Car Porters union, the first African American union in the US.

1920 · Eugene V. Debs runs for president on the Socialist Party ticket. He receives almost 1 million votes while serving a prison sentence for speaking out against World War I.

1924 · National Origins Act. Japanese immigrants are barred from coming to the US and all other incoming groups have severe quotas placed on immigration. The only exception is the wives of Chinese merchants.[37]

1927 · Creation of Saudi Arabia. After more than 25 years of guerrilla warfare against the Ottoman empire, rival Arab families, and royal families of the Middle East, the Treaty of Jeddah recognizes Abd Al-Aziz ibn Saud as the king of what would be named Saudi Arabia. Since before World War I, Britain and France had made grabs for territory in the Middle East. Before the war, the great prize was the Suez Canal and the access it gives to commercial markets. Between World War I and World War II, however, the British navy converts its engines to oil from coal. The Treaty of Jeddah helps British interests by keeping territory out of the hands of the French or Arabs hostile to Great Britain. Oil is not discovered until the early 30s and isn't exported until 1938. By that time Saudi Arabia is an absolute monarchy and, more or less, a friend of the West.[38]

1930 · National Unemployed Council formed. 1,320 delegates meet in Chicago to create a national organization to respond to the devastation of the Great Depression that began in 1929. The councils mobilize thousands to stop evictions; protect against police brutality as people fight for the necessities of life; stop scabbing during strikes; and

fight for crucial relief programs such as unemployment insurance.

1934 · The Export-Import Bank is created in the US to promote domestic employment. Cheaper credit is made available to those businesses exporting 100% American made goods. In 1987 the Bank agrees to permit 15% foreign content and create a sliding scale that will permit subsidies on goods with up to 50% foreign content.[39]

· **Harry Dexter White authors a study for the US Treasury Department** which will later form the basis of the Bretton Woods agreement. The report proposes an international stabilization fund to stabilize exchange rates and remove controls on currency exchange and establishes an international bank to provide capital for economic reconstruction. These ideas become the International Monetary Fund and World Bank, respectively, through the Bretton Woods agreement.[40]

· **The Tydings-McDuffie Act** reduces Filipino immigration to 50 people per year. This quota stays in effect until 1946.[41]

· **Southern Textile Strike.** In the fall, 325,000 textile workers in the South go on strike. Six years before, textiles workers, mostly women of the Gastonia mills of North Carolina, struck. Working with the Trade Union Education League, a precursor to the CIO, thousands of workers fought pitch battles with police and several were killed, including the beloved Ella May Wiggins. Again, violence is the response of the government, particularly in South Carolina. The workers respond with flying squadrons to rapidly spread the strike, picketing, battling with police and guards, and entering mills to dismantle machinery. Within weeks the strike builds to over 421,000 textile workers. Thirteen workers are killed, thousands of others arrested and beaten. Using the newly passed Wagner Act (see below), President Roosevelt sets up a mediation board and the strike is called off. By the end of 1935, more than 1.5 million workers go on strike.

1935 · Formation of the Congress of Industrial Organizations (CIO). The American Federation of Labor (AFL) has around 3 million members in 1935, mostly in skilled trades, and is slow to respond to the militancy of industrial workers. John L. Lewis of the United Mine Workers stages a confrontation with AFL leaders at the '35 convention and the CIO is born. Within six months it has 2+ million members and is formally expelled from the AFL in 1936. For years the CIO withstands red-baiting and rallies under the banner "Organize the Unorganized." The CIO fights for the Social Security Act, the Minimum Wage Law, and unemployment insurance.

· **The Wagner Act** extends the Bill of Rights (freedom of speech, press, and assembly) to American labor whose most radical elements are already repressed and destroyed. The right to organize, enter into contracts and strike are extended primarily to industrial workers. However, it excludes large sectors of the working class, e.g., agricultural workers (where most Blacks and Latinos work), restaurant workers, and government workers.

1936 · Keynesianism Developed. John Maynard Keynes writes The General Theory of Employment, Interest and Money. He argues that the free market creates unemployment and that profitability is linked to reducing labor costs by cutting wages and automation. He also argues that unemployment leads to a ruined economy and that governments should actively intervene in the economy by spending on public works and direct financial support to the unemployed.[42]

1936-1939 · Spanish Civil War. After the military, led by Francisco Franco, attempts to take control of the country, a country-wide insurrection stops the coup. A coalition of nationalist, communist and anarchist unions, and peasant organizations wages a 3-year struggle. Germany supports the fascists with arms and air support. Europe wants to prevent revolution. With the exception of the USSR, none rally around the effort. Even the Soviet Union's support is conditional on building alliances with other European countries. Differences in strategy weaken the revolutionary forces, and they turn on each other. The effort is defeated and the fascists control Spain.

1937 · International Brigades. Workers from around the world form brigades to help the Spanish defeat fascism. The Abraham Lincoln Brigade is formed in the US. Thousands of Americans smuggle themselves out of the country to fight in Spain.

1938 · Fair Labor Standards Act. Campaigns by unions, the unemployed, and other workers leads to the Fair Labor Standards Act (FLSA). It establishes the minimum wage at 25 cents per hour and a 40-hour work week.

1939-1945 · World War II. A deep depression in Germany (brought about by the Allied demand for reparations from the Central powers after WW I) and increasing nationalism sees the rise of fascism. The desire to rebuild the German colonial empire is a direct attack on Britain's and France's colonial holdings. In the East, Japan also develops a fascist state with a desire for colonial expansion. The 20 year attempt by Britain and the US to keep that expansion in check (including restrictions on Japanese trade and shipping) fail. War is the result. At the end of six years, however, the US and the USSR become the new world superpowers.[43]

1941 · The Atlantic Charter. President Franklin D. Roosevelt and British Prime Minister Winston Churchill meet at the historic Atlantic Conference where the Charter is created. Meeting in great secrecy aboard two ships, the two leaders discuss the general strategy of the war against the Axis Powers (Germany, Japan & Italy). They declare the Atlantic Charter on August 14, 1941, which says, among other things, that the powers want no colonies and that they respect the right of all peoples to choose their government. This promise is made specifically to insure the support of colonized people against the Axis.

· **A. Philip Randolph organizes an all African-American March on Washington to desegregate federal jobs.** Three days before the march, President Roosevelt issues Executive Order 8802, establishing the Committee on Fair Employment and ending racial discrimination in government jobs.

1942 · Japanese-Americans Interned. After the US declares war on Japan, 2,000 Japanese community leaders along the Pacific Coast states and Hawaii are rounded up and interned in Department of Justice camps.

· **Bracero Program.** Because of US demands for agricultural labor during World War II, the United States and Mexico sign a treaty for the recruitment and employment of Mexican citizens. Lured by promises of good wages, farmworkers serve terms of employment where they have almost no rights & are paid miserable sums. After their labor is used the workers are sent back to Mexico. The program, known as the Bracero Program, officially ends on

May 30, 1963 but the agricultural workers continue coming into the United States until 1964.

1943 · Wendell L. Wilkie, the conservative Republican presidential nominee in 1940, writes the book One World. It details how, after WW II, "race imperialism" of European colonialism and American racism would be confronted. This book marks a shift in US politics away from isolationism towards interdependence.[44]

1944 · International Monetary and Financial Conference of the United & Associated Nations (Bretton Woods). In 1941, as part of the US aid to Great Britain, the British government is forced to commit to supporting the US position on international financial arrangements. This debt is called in at the Bretton Woods conference where the World Bank and the International Monetary Fund is created. The IMF is first mandated to regulate an international monetary system to facilitate global trade. However, governments are to remain in charge of their own financial policies. Today the IMF now lends to countries in economic crisis & requires severe changes in economic policy including a reduced money supply & government spending, privatization, and removing restrictions on capital flows.[45]

1945 · Dumbarton Oaks Proposal. A proposal written by the "Great Powers" concerning an international organization. The participants — Great Britain, the Soviet Union, the United States and China — see an organization with a prominent Security Council, a weak General Assembly, an emphasis on states rather than individuals, and a right to colonialism. Human rights is mentioned only once in the text and reflects only social and economic cooperation.

· Inter-American Conference on Problems of War & Peace. A conference of 20 nations in Chapultepec Castle in Mexico City is called as a reaction to the Dumbarton Oaks Proposal. Attendees contend that if the crusade of World War II was in the name of democratic principles, then the new international organization should be based on democracy. The delegates state that the Dumbarton Oaks plan needs to be improved and endorse a list of fundamental principles they desire to have applied to the future peace.

· United Nations Conference on International Organization. Held in San Francisco, this meeting is the founding conference for the United Nations. Almost 300 delegates attend with 2,500 advisors. Never before have groups and individuals not part of a government exerted such influence on an international meeting. The US alone invites 42 NGOs (non-governmental organizations) to send consultants. The US, Britain, and the Soviet Union work together to stick with the Dumbarton Oaks plan, but international popular pressure forces a compromise. On June 26, 1945, the UN Charter is signed by all delegates.

· All-Colonial People's Conference. Within days of the signing of the UN Charter, the Pan-African Federation, the Federation of Indian Associations in Britain, the West African Students' Union, the Ceylon Students' Association, and the Burma Association partner to organize a conference. Using the language of the UN Charter, they demand self-determination and racial equality.

· Fifth Pan-African Congress. Representatives from more than 20 countries in Africa, the Caribbean and the Americas meet in Manchester, England in October. Inspired by the All-Colonial People's Conference, the delegates demand independence, an end to racial discrimination and respect for human rights. In a resolution called "The Challenge to Colonial Powers" they agree to organize politically, in trade unions and, if necessary, to engage in armed struggle. "The Delegates to the Fifth Pan-African Congress believe in peace....Yet if the Western world is still determined to rule mankind by force, then Africans, as a last resort, may have to appeal to force in the effort to achieve Freedom, even if force destroys the world."

1946 · Genocide Convention. Issued on December 11, 1946, the Convention on the Prevention and Punishment of the Crime of Genocide makes genocide a crime under international law. The Convention defines genocide as any number of acts committed with intent to destroy, in whole or in part, a national, ethnic, racial, or religious group.

1946-1947 · The Taft-Hartley Act is passed to repeal the Wagner Labor Act (National Labor Relations Act) and return workers to the money-hungry horrors of the merciless National Association of Manufacturers and the Chambers of Commerce. The Act prevents strikes and so-called secondary boycotts (a measure that will be used against the 1955 Montgomery Bus Boycott). The Taft-Hartley Act has its roots in anti-communism and is justified as a "cold war" measure against the organizing of workers, especially the CIO.

1946-1953 · Operation Dixie. The Congress of Industrial Organizations launches "Operation Dixie," a mass organizing project in the South. Most industrial workers exist in towns created by and for the companies that employ them. Despite moments of resistance, unionization is still isolated in the old Confederacy. The Taft-Hartley Act, in combination with the Republican backlash against labor, stall out the drive. After seven years, Operation Dixie ends. Although it organizes more than 600,000 workers over the course of the project, historians generally agree it is a failure.

1947 · GATT. With World War II ending, the US wants a post-war system based on expanding trade. The General Agreement on Tariffs & Trade is created out of the Bretton Woods conference. Member nations of the treaty agree to give no special trade status to one member that isn't given to all. This treaty, in 1995, leads to the World Trade Organization.[46]

· Marshall Plan. During a Harvard commencement, Secretary of State George Marshall proposes to supply capital to European economies. This would enable them to rebuild and to become capable military allies of the US against the USSR.[47]

· W.E.B. Du Bois, at almost 80 years old, supervises the creation of a document for the NAACP detailing the United States' history of racial discrimination and its obligations under the UN Charter. When members of the Commission on Human Rights are deluged by thousands of letters from around the world requesting help on human rights issues, UN member governments have representatives publicly state the committee has no power to take action on individual cases. Still, Du Bois presents the Commission with *An Appeal to the World: A Statement on the Denial of Human Rights to Minorities in the Case of Citizens of Negro Descent in the United States of America and An Appeal to the United Nations for Redress*. News of the report spreads around the world and is used by Asian and African delegates in arguing for an end to colonial empires.

· The Truman Doctrine. President Truman declares that the world must choose between "freedom or totalitarianism" by which he means capitalism or socialism/communism. This signals a rising tension between the US and the Soviet Union that will lead to the Cold War.

1948 · Beginning of the Cold War. In 1945 both the US and the USSR have *reichsmarks* (German currency) plates and print currency. Russia uses its *reichsmarks* to purchase millions of dollars worth of goods in the western zone of Germany. The West responds by declaring the Soviet-printed currency unacceptable. Cigarettes become the *de facto* currency (1 carton of Lucky Strikes = $2300). Under Operation Bird Dog the US replaces *reichsmarks* with *deutschemarks*, printed only in Washington DC. The USSR sees this as a plan to set up a western German government in opposition to communism. On the day the *deutschemarks* go into circulation, the Soviet Union blockades Berlin.[48]

· Universal Declaration of Human Rights. Viewed as a vision statement, the Declaration covers five areas of human rights: civil, political, social, economic, and cultural. The Commission doesn't want the Declaration to be a narrow document, and therefore frames it as a declaration of principles. The rights within are to be widely understood and then serve as an inspiration for action.

· Creation of Israel. Before WW II, France and Britain had basically controlled the entire Middle East. Battles during the war, however, lead to the independence of several countries in the region including Syria and Lebanon. After the war, Britain finds itself unable to propose a settlement that will satisfy Jews and Arabs while also insuring Western oil interests. On May 14, Britain leaves Palestine, the state of Israel is declared, and millions of Palestinians are ultimately displaced. This displacement gives rise to the current Palestinian struggle against Israel for a homeland.[49]

· Organization of American States. After the US and Great Britain introduce the Dumbarton Oaks Proposal on the formation of the United Nations, nations around the world begin organizing alternatives. The Dumbarton Proposal called for a single security council with limited membership. In response, Latin American countries form the Organization of American States. The institution contains a single General Assembly, an elected secretary-general and three councils to work on various programs. Although dominated by the US, the OAS does provide an alternative vision of international cooperation.[50]

1949 · Chinese Revolution. After more than 20 years of hostilities, the Chinese Communist Party led by Mao Zedung defeats the nationalist forces led by Chiang Kai-shek and founds the People's Republic of China. The nationalists were forced to retreat to the island of Taiwan where the Republic of China is established. Although both forces ceased hostilities during the Japanese invasion of China, fighting begins almost immediately after the war. The Communist Party leads a guerrilla campaign against the nationalists who are aided by Western governments. China's experience during the revolution, including profound ideological disagreements with the Communist Party of the USSR, leads it to develop different theories of revolution, development, and imperialism. Maoism, as the Chinese application of Marxism has come to be called, places great significance on imperialism by developed countries. The need to resist imperialism - as well ideas of permanent revolution, agricultural collectivism, and the importance of the peasantry - are central to Maoism and have greatly influenced liberation struggles around the world.[51]

· NATO Formed. Although industrialized Western countries such as the US and Great Britain were forced to modify their view of the United Nations by international pressure, they do create a military alliance outside the international structure of the UN. NATO (North Atlantic Treaty Organization) is dominated by the US and since the public reason for its existence is to counter the Soviet threat in Eastern Europe, membership is limited to European countries. Even when the Soviet Union collapses, NATO's existence is assured. With a military alliance that doesn't have to answer to any countries in the Global South, European countries and the US are free to use military force to pacify countries of the former Soviet Bloc as well as threaten nationalists within Russia.[52]

1950 · McCarran Internal Security Act. Members of the American Communist Party and others are forced to register with the US Attorney General's office. The bill passes over President Truman's veto and uses the internment of Japanese Americans during World War II as a precedent for the mass

detainment of alleged subversives. Millions of people lose their jobs as a result of the paranoia.[53]

1950-1953 · The Korean War. The first war after World War II under the pretext to eliminate, or if not possible to contain, communist governments. The undeclared war, legally a "police action," is also a result of anti-communism and cold war hysteria aimed at curtailing labor organizing. Organized labor capitulates to business during this period. A new economic theory develops that the war industry relieves US economic depressions.

1952 · The McCarran-Walter Act. Congress replaces the Asiatic Barred Zone, established under the 1917 Immigration Act, with the Asia-Pacific Triangle. This caps immigration from the East to 2000 people per year. However, those of Asian descent born in other countries are counted under this quota. This system stays in place until 1965.[54]

· Egyptian Coup. 89 members of the Free Officers' Movement, a secret society of military officers led by Gamal Abd al-Nasser, topples the monarchy of King Farouk. Originally Minister of the Interior, Nasser becomes president in 1954 and serves until his death in 1970. During the early part of his presidency he urges independent movements throughout Africa. Mildly socialist, Nasser encourages other African countries to seek independence from colonialism. At home he represses the Muslim Brotherhood, an Islamic fundamentalist organization which makes an assassination attempt. Nasser's influence on African independence movements wanes by the late 1960s.[55]

1953 · Shah Restored to Power in Iran. Despite being elected by a large majority in parliament, a US and British operation helps overthrow the government of Prime Minister Mossadegh and restore the Shah. Mossadegh's plan to nationalize the British-owned oil company brings the wrath of the colonial powers. The Shah's reign of repression and torture lasts 25 years, but the oil industry remains foreign-owned (40% to British companies, 40% to US, and 20% others).[56]

1954 · *Brown vs. Board of Education*. The Supreme Court strikes down separate but equal doctrine from *Plessy vs. Ferguson* as unconstitutional.

· **Puerto Rican *Independistas* Attack Congress.**
On March 14, Rafael Cancel Miranda, Irving Flores, Andres Cordero, and Lolita Lebron enter the US House of Representatives armed and holding the Puerto Rican flag. They open fire on the US Congress. Lebron, after being released in 1979 from prison, represents the Puerto Rican independence movement before the UN Decolonization Committee.

1955 · Formation of the Third World.
Representatives from more than 29 countries meet in Bandung, Indonesia to develop a vision of the world separate from the Soviet East or the US/European West. Their vision, based on a philosophy of radical humanism, comes to be known as the Bandung World. Since it is advanced as a third way, the countries behind it become collectively known as the Third World.[57]

· **AFL-CIO Merger.** After the passage of the anti-union Taft-Hartley that effectively brought most organizing to a halt in the South, and after the purge of most independent and pro-Communist unions from their ranks, the AFL and CIO merge. This, combined with a huge post-war boom, solidifies business unionism in the US.

1955-1956 · Montgomery Bus Boycott. The US economy rapidly expanded after WW II. On the one hand, industry was anxious to expand South but found strict segregation an obstacle to the assembly line. On the other hand, the hopes and expectations of African-Americans in the South were rising with prosperity all around them and the success internationally of people of color against colonialism. In 1955, the Women's Political Caucus, the NAACP, as well as unions and Black churches organize a bus boycott in Montgomery, Alabama — thus begins the modern civil rights movement. The bus boycott mobilizes thousands in the city to walk or car pool to work and participation is nearly 100%. In 1956, the Supreme Court outlaws segregation on local bus lines.

1956-1990 · African Independence Struggles.
Although African people had resisted colonial rule from the beginning, after World War II the movement gained significant momentum. The European colonies support the Allies throughout the war by providing bases, troops, and, most importantly, not allying with the Axis powers. In return, the promise of Europe and the US (in the Atlantic Charter) was independence after the war. However, this did-

n't materialize. The struggle for independence takes various forms, including armed struggle, the majority of independence is achieved by mass actions (i.e. general strikes, demonstrations, boycotts, etc.). As the world's economic structure changes, colonial powers no longer desire (or can afford) a permanent military presence to maintain control. Beginning as early as the 1950s, colonialism begins to take a new form of financial domination of the local political & economic structure (neocolonialism). In many countries in Africa, this means monarchies, puppet regimes, or (in the case of southern Africa) white minority rule. Therefore resistance to colonialization links opposition to the colonial political structure with opposition to the economic structure. In a more refined manner, the international financial system remains the primary tool of neocolonialization.[58]

1958 · The European Economic Community (Common Market) is formed. European countries form the Common Market, as it becomes commonly known, with the goal of creating a free trade area among member nations with free movement of labor and capital. It also establishes common tariffs to goods from outside Europe.[59]

1958 & 1959 · Silicon Chip. Jack Kilby, of Texas Instruments, and Robert Noyce, of Fairchild Semiconductor, independently invent the silicon chip. This invention will completely change the way production is handled. By the 1970s automation, use of computer technology in production, leads to enormous productivity increases with a smaller workforce.[60]

1959 · Cuban Revolution. Students, workers, farmers, and other segments of society join in with the July 10th Movement led by Che Guevara and Fidel Castro. After a 3 year guerrilla war, the dictator Fulgencio Batista is ousted and a socialist government established. While not initially hostile to the US, despite Washington's backing of Batista, the Revolution's programs of nationalizing industries (including the giant sugar plantations), public health, education and housing alarm the US. Washington establishes an embargo of the island and Cuba seeks an alliance with the Soviet Union. In 1961, the US attempts to topple the government when CIA-trained counter-revolutionaries invade Cuba at the Bay of Pigs. Cuba repulses the attempted US invasion.[61]

1959-1978 · Latin American Revolutions. Latin American resistance to grinding poverty and inequality as well as the more than century-old US policy of intervention converge. 19th century struggles against imperialism were led by the colonial aristocracy and did not challenge the rule of political elites native to the colonies. 20th century struggle against imperialism is synonymous with resistance to global capitalism. These struggles are against rule by economic and political elites. This resistance takes various forms from social revolutions in Cuba (1959) and Nicaragua (1979) to electoral revolutions in Chile (1970) to guerrilla campaigns in Bolivia (1952-1964) and El Salvador. In every case, conservative elements in the country ally with multinational corporations and the US government in an attempt to roll back social gains and crush popular movements.

1960 · Founding of OPEC. Five countries (Venezuela, Iran, Iraq, Kuwait, and Saudi Arabia) meet in Baghdad, Iraq. Hoping to cooperate to control the supply and price of oil, they form the Organization of Petroleum Exporting Countries (OPEC). Sometimes referred to as a "union of producers," it is hoped OPEC will give developing countries some leverage against the oil companies based in the developed countries. Within 15 years 8 additional countries join.[62] In 1973 the OPEC nations and oil companies reach an impasse on oil prices and a crisis occurs when the price of crude oil is increased by 200%. Since the "energy crisis" the influence of OPEC has declined due mostly to the appearance of non-OPEC oil producers such as Norway and Alaska.[63]

1960-Present · Neocolonialism in Africa. Beginning with the destabilization of the Congo in 1960, colonial powers in Africa use covert violence in addition to financial domination. The Republic of Congo achieved independence from Belgium in 1960. Patrice Lumumba, the first Prime Minister, is a socialist and anti-imperialist with a pan-African vision. In 1961, he is assassinated by Belgium with US complicity. In the years that follow political assassinations, coup d'etats, and economic destabilization become the norm in country after country as anti-colonial struggles throughout the continent heat up. In many instances, such as the coup in Ghana against socialist and pan-Africanist Kwame Nkrumah, Western governments in general and the

US specifically are the cause. Western governments also increasingly use economic aid and trade as a means of maintaining control. At first, as in the case of Ghana, countries like the US and Britain would limit or threaten to cut off financial aid if social programs did not meet with their approval. However, the rise of international financial institutions (IMF and World Bank) has meant a decreased need for military action (except in special circumstances) and the ability to use international trade as a weapon of neo-colonialism. By the time South African people's movements end apartheid in 1991, the mechanisms of globalization are able to dictate terms like mass privatization and decreased social spending.[64]

1960-Present · COINTELPROs are the FBI domestic counter-intelligence programs developed to destroy individuals and organizations considered to be politically objectionable by the FBI. The primary target of COINTELPRO in this period is the Black Power Movement, especially the Black Panther Party (BPP). The assassination of Black Panther Fred Hampton, the violent police attack on anti-Vietnam War and Black radical demonstrators at the 1968 Democratic Convention in Chicago, the incarceration and eventual assassination of BPP field marshal George Jackson, the incarceration of Geronimo ji Jaga (Pratt) in San Quentin (released in 1997), and the arrest & imprisonment of Assata Shakur (now living in exile in Cuba) and Sundiata Acoli, represent some major cases of state repression in this period. Other recent cases include the targeting of those involved in the Civil Rights Movement, First Nation organizations like the American Indian Movement (AIM), and Central American solidarity groups during the 1980s.

1962 · SDS Formed. Students involved with the League for Industrial Democracy meet in Port Huron, Michigan. At the end of the meeting the students publish the *Port Huron Statement* which becomes the symbolic break between the Old Left and the New Left.

1963 · Organization of African Unity. After years of fighting for freedom from imperialism, the heads of 32 independent African countries meet in Addis Ababa, Ethiopia and sign the charter for the Organization of African Unity. After World War II, the people of the world felt betrayed by the US and Europe's refusal to abandon colonialism. Many

Project South: Institute for the Elimination of Poverty & Genocide

countries in Africa wage and win wars for independence. The OAU is established as a continent-wide institution for cooperation and pushing colonialism out of Africa.[65]

1965 · Vietnam War. This conflict further sharpens all American foreign policy in terms of the Cold War with the implementation of the so-called Domino Theory. The theory holds that if one country becomes communist in a region more will follow and thus close markets to capitalism. Vietnam had successfully fought off decades of foreign intervention. The French were forced to concede Vietnam in 1954 and moved to the South of the country with the promise of free elections in two years. The US intervened by financially setting up the Diem administration in the South. President Kennedy, and later President Johnson, began committing troops, using the fraudulent Gulf of Tonken incident, and escalating the war. By the end of the war, 1,700,000 Vietnamese people are killed, 50,000 American soldiers are killed, 250,000 wounded and over 7 million tons of bombs dropped (about one 500-pound bomb for every Vietnamese person). By 1971, 65% of the American people oppose the war. The anti-war movement radicalize an entire generation. This activity, coupled with the returning Black working class veteran, changes the nature of movement politics in the US.

· **Grape Boycott.** Cesar Chavez, Dolores Huerta, and others lead members of the Farm Workers' Association in a strike against California grape growers. The Farm Workers' Association will become the United Farm Workers (UFW).

1966 · International Covenant on Civil & Political Rights (ICCPR). The ICCPR is adopted on December 16, 1966 and goes into effect on March 26, 1976. The ICCPR gives much of the Universal Declaration of Human Rights a binding legal force. The Covenant outlines individual rights including the right to life (art. 6); fair trial rights (art. 14); freedom of movement and freedom to choose a residence (art. 12); freedom of opinion and expression (art. 19); freedom of thought, conscience and religion (art. 18); freedom of association (art. 22), and democratic rights, equality rights and rights of minorities. The ICCPR prohibits slavery (art. 8); arbitrary arrest or detention (art. 9); and torture and cruel, inhuman or degrading treatment or punishment (art. 7). The Covenant creates an imple-

mentation body, the Human Rights Committee, composed of 18 experts. However, the treaty breaks up 5 areas of human rights (civil, political, economic, social, and cultural). This is an attack on universality - the idea that all areas of human rights must be respected at once - and a victory for governments, like the US, that don't acknowledge the existence of economic, social, and cultural rights.

· **International Covenant on Economic, Social & Cultural Rights (ICESCR).** The ICESCR is adopted on December 16, 1966, and enters into force on March 26, 1976. As with the ICCPR, the International Covenant on Economic, Social and Cultural Rights (ICESCR) gives many of the norms of the Universal Declaration of Human Rights a binding legal force. The ICESCR recognizes the rights to work that is freely chosen (art. 6); to the enjoyment of just and favorable conditions of work (art. 7); to form and join trade unions (art. 8); to social security, including social insurance (art. 9); to protection and assistance for the family, especially mothers, children, and youth (art. 10); and to an adequate standard of living, including adequate food, clothing and housing (art. 11). The US government has steadfastly refused to accept the existence of economic, social & cultural rights.

· **The Black Panther Party** for Self Defense (BPP) is founded in Oakland, CA. The symbol of the black panther originates with a Lowndes County, AL organization formed in the early 60s. The BPP blends ideas of Black nationalism, armed self-defense, and the philosophies of Marx, Mao, and Franz Fanon. The Black Panther Party adopts a "Ten Point Platform" which includes demands for freedom, an end to police brutality, bread, housing, land and peace.

1967 · National Welfare Rights Organization formed. For nine years, the NWRO organizes tens of thousands of welfare recipients to reject the stigma of welfare and demand income, food, and justice. Membership peaks at 22,000 families in chapters in every state.

1968 · The American Indian Movement (AIM) is founded in Minnesota. The organization is patterned after the Black Panther Party's community self-defense model.

1969 · Stonewall. Tired of continuing police harassment, working-class transgender bar hoppers lead a 4-day rebellion of queer people of color, later called the Stonewall Rebellion, when the bar is again raided by police. The NY sixth precinct had routinely raided gay bars in the area, harassing patrons and owners. After the rebellion, rallies and demonstrations are held throughout New York and help form the Gay Liberation Front.

1970s · Working Harder for Less. From the late 1970s to 1990, US manufacturing productivity increases 35%. Wages are stagnant or fall in real terms.[66]

1970-Present · Struggle for Vieques. Puerto Rican organizations call for the removal of the US Navy from the island of Vieques, a small community subject to testing of live ordinance (including depleted uranium) which has degraded the environment and may contribute to abnormally high cancer rates. The protest culminates in mass demonstrations and a year-long occupation of the bomb site by more than 200 activists.

1971-1991 · Multinational Corporations Gain While Workers Lose. Sales of the 500 largest multinational corporations grows from $721 billion in 1971 to $5.2 trillion in 1991. The number of workers they employ remains fairly constant at 26 million.[67]

· Attica Prison Uprising. More than 1,000 inmates take over a prison yard at the Attica prison in upstate NY and at least 12 prisoners are killed. This uprising sparks a wave of organizing among prisoners and gives national attention to the struggle for prisoners' rights.

· *Ms.* Magazine is founded, serving as the first major magazine to discuss social, political, and economic issues affecting women, including abortion, domestic violence and equal wages for equal work.

1973 · Rise of Neoliberalism. Faced with rising inflation and a staggering economy, President Nixon abandons the commitment made at the Bretton Woods conference in 1944 which linked the US dollar to gold. This had established a fixed rate of exchange, but currency is now free to seek its own exchange rate. From this point on, the neoliberal philosophy grows in dominance.[68]

· The Trilateral Commission. Created in 1973 by economic and political elites in the US, Western Europe, and Japan, the Commission coordinates and advocates corporate concerns. It serves as an international lobbying force for neoliberalism.

1974 · Declarations of Principles for the New International Economic Order (NIEO). Newly independent colonies in Africa, Asia and Latin America begin demanding a more just global economic system between nations. A collection of progressive intellectuals and politicians argues for better trade terms since the free market, left alone, would never reduce global inequalities.[69]

1976 · Orlando Letelier and Ronni Moffitt are murdered in Washington, D.C. Letelier, former Chilean foreign and defence minister, was in exile and with 2 American citizens were killed by agents of the Chilean dictatorship of Augusto Pinochet with US complicity.

· *Buckley v. Valeo*. The US Supreme Court rules that unlimited amounts of private contributions to political campaigns is equal to free speech, overturning Congress' 1974 amendments to the Federal Elections Campaign Act that limited campaign contributions. The amendments are upheld by the US Court of Appeals for the D.C. Circuit.

1977 · Anti-Gay Feelings Begin to be Used as a Wedge Issue. Bisexual activist Alan Rockaway co-authors the nation's first successful gay rights ordinance put to public vote. Dade County, Florida passes the ordinance, but after an extremely homophonic counter campaign called "Save Our Children" featuring Anita Bryant, the ordinance is repealed.

1979 · First lesbian, gay, bisexual, and transgender (LGBT) March on Washington draws 100,000 people to march for basic human rights.

1980s · In Poland, Solidarity fights for free trade unions, autonomy of workers, and self-management. Warsaw Steelworks is site of the main strike. In 1997, the Steelworks is owned by an Italian Conglomerate.[70]

· Germany and France abandon capital controls. Money can now travel across their borders unhindered.

1980 · Computer Processing Power Explodes.
Maximum computer RAM (random access memory) is 64k. In 1990 the maximum is 4 mb, an increase of 65 million percent.[71] Computer processing power grows so powerful that how people work is completely changed.

1980 · 'President' Moi of Kenya signs formal agreement with United States for use of military facilities. Although ex-president Moi is widely viewed as a corrupt dictator and frequent abuser of human rights, his agreement with the United States has allowed US military personnel to operate within Kenya as launching ground in East Africa.

1981-1982 · The World Bank and the International Monetary Fund initiate Structural Adjustment Programs (SAPs). Developing countries of the South are forced to adopt measures including privatization, reduced social spending, and dismantling labor and environmental laws. As the programs become more widespread, the philosophy behind these policies is referred to as "neoliberalism" by popular movements in Africa, Asia, and Latin America. Resistance to neoliberalism serves as a base for an internationally linked movement.

1982 · AIDS. After years of referring to GRID (Gay Related Immune Deficiency), the acronym AIDS (Acquired Immune Deficiency Syndrome) is coined when research reveals that the disease is not gay-related. The stigma, however, remains and the US federal government continues to underfund research. President Ronald Reagan has yet to publicly acknowledge the disease. By the late 1990s, AIDS infects millions worldwide and threatens Africa with another form of genocide.

1983 · US invasion of Grenada. President Reagan uses longstanding US hostility with Grenada in an attempt to whip up Congressional support for a covert war in Central America. In 1979 the New Jewel Movement (NJM) led by Maurice Bishop overthrew the dictatorship of Eric Gairy. The NJM established a People's Revolutionary Government based on revolutionary socialist principles. The new government stepped up criticism of US foreign policy while there was an internal conflict within the NJM. In October of '79, Bishop was placed under house arrest and eventually executed by an internal faction. This action led the prime ministers of Dominica and Jamaica to call for US intervention, although it is accepted this was done simply to

curry favor with the US government. This call, along with the presence of 200 Cuban advisors in Grenada, provides Reagan the public reason he needs to invade.[72]

· Caribbean Basin Initiative. After experimenting with neoliberal forms in Puerto Rico, Mexico, and other Latin American countries, the Reagan administration establishes a program which provides direct federal aid to Caribbean countries establishing free trade zones and ending tariffs for goods coming into the US. The program is a profit bonanza for US-based companies and their subsidiaries since they are encouraged to relocate production to the Caribbean where wages are lower, unions crushed and corporate taxes almost non-existent. The framework of the CBI becomes the framework for later neoliberal treaties and programs.[73]

1984 · Eastern and Western tribes of the Cherokee Nation hold a reunion at Red Clay, Tennessee. This is the first meeting of the tribes since the 1838 Removal separated them.

· New Zealand Structurally Adjusts Itself. With the presidency and parliament in the hands of the Labor Party, New Zealand adopts all of the policies of structural adjustment. Convinced this path will lead to greater economic growth and reduce the country's poverty level, the government willingly adopts policy changes other countries have fought bitterly against. In comparison with Australia, which shares similar growth patterns, the changes hurt New Zealand deeply. According to a New Zealand professor, the changes cost the country NZ $114 billion (or NZ $30,000 for each citizen). Worker productivity in Australia, previously equal to New Zealand, increases 4 times faster. However, the top 10% income earners see a 26.5% increase in real income in less than 15 years. During the same period the poorest 50% of the population see a decline in their purchasing power.

1986-1994 · Uruguay Round of GATT Talks. The GATT (General Agreement on Tariffs and Trade), a treaty designed to loosen international trade restrictions, is updated during multi-year "rounds" of negotiation. The 7th round begins with some developed countries wanting greater enforcement of the treaty. As the eight-year negotiations end in Morocco, the World Trade Organization (WTO) is formed. With the official status as an international organization, more than 140 member states in

2002, and a newly expanded mandate far greater than GATT, the WTO is the enforcer of corporate globalization.[74]

1986 · Mexico adopts the "Washington Consensus." The federal government of Mexico officially adopts neoliberalism by instituting mass privatization, deregulation of the financial markets, reduction of government subsidies, relaxing trade barriers, and signing GATT.[75]

· IMF Structural Adjustment Facility. Although the International Monetary Fund had forced debtor nations to make changes in their economy (like devaluing the currency and cutting government spending) since the 70s, the process becomes formal. US Treasury Secretary James Baker introduces the "Baker Plan." This makes structural adjustment a condition of the loan and expands the reach. In 1989 the World Bank follows. The transfer of wealth from the Global South to the Global North expands.[76]

1987 · Reparations for Japanese-Americans. The House of Representatives votes to make an official apology to Japanese-Americans interned during World War II and pay each surviving internee $20,000. A year later the Senate also votes yes. President Bush signs the program into law in 1989.

· Outraged by the government's mismanagement of the AIDS crisis, ACT-UP (AIDS Coalition to Unleash Power) is formed in New York. Three weeks later, ACT-UP organizes a Wall Street demonstration where 17 people are arrested protesting profiteering by pharmaceutical companies.

· Intifadah. Arabic for abrupt and sudden waking up from sleep or unconcerned status, the Intifadah describes the explosion of tension by Palestinians in about 50 towns and villages in the West Bank and Gaza Strip (the Occupied Territories). Beginning in December 1987 and lasting through 1988, young Palestinians protest the Israeli occupation with stones and slings and Israeli troops respond with increased repression. 300 Palestinians are killed in 1988 alone. However, Israel's heavy handed response to the uprising brings greater international pressure for a peaceful solution. Although a peace plan is eventually reached, it doesn't last. A second Intifadah begins in 2000 and reaches a crisis level in 2002.[77]

1989 · Fall of the Berlin Wall. As corporate globalization speeds up the Soviet Bloc can no longer defend against the capitalist onslaught. When the Berlin Wall falls many economists view it as the "end of history." In short, that the debate on economic theory is over. However, the growing worldwide movement against corporate globalization shows otherwise.

· The National Welfare Rights Union, the National Union of the Homeless and the National Anti-Hunger Coalition gather in Philadelphia at the first Up & Out of Poverty Now! Summit. This gathering launches a campaign to build organizations led by low-income people to fight for basic survival and dignity.

1989-1994 · Working Even Harder for Even Less. Output per hour in non-farm businesses increases by almost 10%. Wages per hour increase by less than 4%.[78]

1990-1997 · Global South Pays the North. The countries of the Global South (what used to be referred to as the Third World) receive a total of $132 billion in new loans, but pay out $160 billion in debt service (interest plus repayment). From 1990 to 1997 the South pays the countries and banks of the North $77 billion more than it receives.[79]

1991 · Global Corporations. 157 of the 500 largest corporations are US-based. 168 are based in Europe and 119 in Japan. In 1971, 280 of the 500 were US based.[80]

· International elite profit from global trade. International bank loans reach $3.6 trillion, foreign exchange reaches $1.2 trillion, and the amount of global publicly traded financial assets reaches $24 trillion. The world's financial trading, however, is conducted by 30-50 banks and some major brokerages.[81]

· Environmental Justice Movements. Spearheaded by the Gulfcoast Tenants' Association and supported by the United Church of Christ - Commission for Racial Justice (UCC-CRJ), the first National People of Color Environmental Leadership Summit is convened. The UCC-CRJ had been working on this issue since 1982, and UCC-CRJ Charles Lee had compiled and analyzed some startling statistics: Government policy stipulates that a preponderance of toxic waste dumps and other environmentally hazardous operations be dumped in communities of color and that many environmental protection groups, including so-called progressive groups, are racist in hiring practices, policies, and operations. There is obvious collusion of so-called environment protection groups with captains in the pollution industries. The fact that one slogan, "Not in My Backyard (NIMBY)," had to undergo intense struggle by people of color to transform the slogan to "Not in Anybody's Backyard (NAMBY)," demonstrated racist narrowness of this purported radical movement. Over 2,000 people of color attend the first Summit. A position paper and a statement of operating principles are adopted.

· **Gulf War.** After US Ambassador April Glaspie assures Iraqi dictator Saddam Hussein that the US has no opinion on border conflicts with Kuwait, Hussein invades the country. The Bush administration believes Iraq, a long-time US ally, would only claim the Rumalyah oil fields. When Iraq occupies the entire country, a multinational force led by the US is assembled to destroy Iraq. As the only remaining superpower, the US is able to use its economic and military muscle to force its way. The Gulf War lasts only weeks, but results in the death of more than 500,000 children from 10 years of economic sanctions.[82] US arms makers receive millions in new contracts. In addition, for the first time in Islamic history and in direct violation to Islamic law a foreign army is based in the land of Mecca (Saudi Arabia).[83]

1992 · **Global Trade.** 15% of global trade is done in "free market" conditions. 25-30% is government managed (mostly through non-tariff barriers). 40% is managed by multinational corporations (through intrafirm trade among subsidiaries).[84]

· **The New Wedge Issue.** Race has been used to divide workers since the beginning of capitalism. With the breaking of the social contract and speed up of neoliberalism, the right wing in the US uses sexual identity as a new wedge issue to divide workers, dismantle the gains of past popular movements, and attack democracy & human rights. In Oregon and Colorado, ballot measures are put to the electorate that equate equal rights for LGBT people as "special rights." The measures attack the language of the civil rights movement while simultaneously asserting that civil rights should be based on

"morality" and "good" behavior. This fosters the idea that there aren't enough resources for everyone, that only some in society deserve those resources, and that undesirable elements (not the ruling elites) are responsible for the scarcity of resources. In effect, this organizes heterosexual people (of all ethnicities) around their heterosexism/homophobia while at the same time enabling the right to move a neoliberal agenda.[85]

1993 · **Kader Industrial Toy Company fire.** The worst industrial fire in the history of capitalism occurs in a toy factory outside Bangkok, Thailand. Although the same factory had 3 or 4 previous fires, no safety precautions were instituted. The last fire destroys the building. With 188 dead and 469 injured, it is the worst since the Triangle Shirtwaist Company factory burned in 1911 killing 146 in New York City.[86]

1994 · **NAFTA.** On January 1 the North American Free Trade Agreement goes into effect. The treaty greatly liberalizes trade between Canada, the US and Mexico with an aim towards ending all tariff barriers by 2010. Activists in Canada and the US are concerned the treaty will allow industry to move production to areas with low wages and little environmental regulation (a concern proved valid in the coming years). Throughout the southern part of Chiapas, Mexico members of the Zapatista Army for National Liberation (EZLN) take over villages on January 1, 1994 to protest neoliberalism's affect on the indigenous people of Mexico.

· **Job Loss Due to Globalization Determined.** Adrian Wood, a professor at the University of Sussex and a former senior economist at the World Bank, publishes a study on job loss. Job loss in advanced economies due to global trade is ten times more than previously thought.[87]

· **Mexican manufacturing productivity increases by 40% since 1980.** However, wages in pesos decreases by 40%.[88]

· **Global Inequality.** A US garment worker can make a shirt in 14 minutes and is paid $7.53. A Bangladeshi worker makes the same shirt in 25 minutes, but is paid only 25 cents per hour. The difference in wages is so great that no matter how productive workers in the Global North are, corporations make greater profits by moving production to the Global South and exploiting workers there.[89]

Project South: Institute for the Elimination of Poverty & Genocide

· **Free Trade Agreement of the Americas.** Secret negotiations for the FTAA begin by all 34 countries of the Western Hemisphere (except Cuba). The goal of the negotiations is to extend NAFTA-like trade agreements throughout the Americas.[90]

· **The US Becomes a Debtor Nation.** Although multinationals and a few individual financiers are winning because of neoliberalism, the nation as a whole is losing. The outflow of financial returns paid to foreign investors on assets held in the US exceeds all profits, dividends, and interest payments collected from investments abroad. This is the first time since 1914 the net sum of earnings on international assets is negative. The US, as a country, is sending more money out then is coming in.[91]

· **GATS Created.** A part of the World Trade Organization, the stated goal of the General Agreement on Trade in Services (GATS) is "progressive liberalization of trade in services." In reality, the treaty is a blueprint for the total privatization of services. The inclusion of GATS in the WTO comes from intensive lobbying by US corporations, particularly American Express and Citicorp. Further negotiations on the agreement are necessary to fully develop it. These negotiations, separate from the WTO round, are to begin in January 2001. They are stalled, however, by the Seattle protests in 1999.[92]

1995 · The United Nations Fourth World Conference on Women. Held in Beijing, China and sponsored by the United Nations, the conference places an emphasis on putting a gender perspective in the "mainstream" of policies and programs in governments and NGOs around the world. The conference calls for a "clear commitment to international norms and standards of equality between men and women." Women's organizations from around the world use this conference to extend victories won in the 1993 human rights conference in Vienna, where international women's organizations moved an agenda that equated women's rights with human rights. They defeated the attacks on universality by China, Saudi Arabia, the US and other countries. The popular movement victory in Vienna was leveraged into ratification of the Convention for the Elimination of Discrimination Against Women (CEDAW) in countries across the globe. At the Fourth World Conference on Women issues including the rights of

queer women, the feminization of poverty, rights to health care and others are all raised during the historic two-week meeting. Although some victories are won – including the recognition for the first time in human history that rape is a war crime – they do not reach the level of Vienna.

· **McNeocolonialism.** There is 1 McDonald's for 40 million Chinese. There is 1 McDonald's for 29,000 Americans.[93]

· **Global Corporations Dominate.** 50% of the US exporting volume comes from 100 companies. 80% from 250 companies. The top 15 exporting firms account for almost 25% of all US manufacturing exports.[94]

· **Mexico Bailout Saves US Corporations.** Mexico enters a deep financial crisis triggered by diminishing reserves of foreign currencies which are needed to redeem short-term debt notes held by international investors. The Mexican federal government devalues the peso in what it believes to be a gradual way. However, foreign investors respond by pulling out, taking $25 billion out of the country. The peso loses 50% of its purchasing power in weeks. The economy contracts by 7%, 1 million jobs are destroyed and wages fall by 33% so debts on houses and cars remain unpaid. This leads to a banking crisis. A $50 billion international bailout stops the bleeding, but the terms of the loan include reduced federal spending, raising taxes and tightening credit & interest rates. These conditions are similar to Structural Adjustment Programs which devastated economies throughout the developing world.[95]

· **El Barzón forms.** As interest rates rise to 130%, Mexican campesinos, small landowners, and business owners in rural and urban areas form a protest movement of debtors. About 500,000 people stop banks from foreclosing, disrupt auctions, and provide legal and technical advice to those hardest hit by the economic crisis.[96]

· **Congress attempts to pass the Foreign Relations Revitalization Act** which seeks to make membership in a group or "advocating terrorism" as a grounds for excluding people from the US. The definition of terrorism is left open. The bill fails.[97]

Project South: Institute for the Elimination of Poverty & Genocide

1996 · Personal Responsibility, Work Opportunity Reconciliation Act (Welfare Reform) Passes. Clinton signs into law a bill to end "welfare as we know it" & throw millions of low-income working moms into the labor market. It eliminates AFDC (Aid to Families with Dependent Children) as an entitlement, sets a five-year lifetime limit for families to receive welfare, institutes mandatory work requirements, and transfers government income support to the states through TANF (Temporary Assistance for Needy Families). Political & economic elites push the false idea that resources will only be given to the "deserving."

· First Intercontinental Encuentro for Humanity and Against Neoliberalism. In the "First Declaration of La Realidad," the Zapatista Army for National Liberation (EZLN) calls for five continental conferences in different regions of the world. The first conference occurs in July-August 1996 in Chiapas. The Second Intercontinental Encuentro for Humanity and Against Neoliberalism takes place in Spain in 1997. Some 3000 people attend from 50 countries to discuss issues surrounding neoliberalism and resistance to it. These grassroots meetings increase the level of understanding of activists from the Global South and raise the awareness of corporate globalization and neoliberalism as an issue for activists from the Global North.[98]

· Brazilians organized the First National Street Children Congress in Brasília. The 500 street children representatives who attended were already experienced with the political process at the state and local levels. The ground-breaking meeting was heavily covered by the media, and the eloquence with which the children spoke captured the attention of the nation.

1997 · General Strike in Haiti. Workers shut down the country for one day demanding that the prime minister suspend negotiations with the IMF/World Bank. The austerity measures imposed by the IMF and World Bank terms would mean 7,000 government workers losing their jobs and the privatization of both the electric and telephone companies.

1998 · Popular Movement Victory Over the MAI. After three years of secret negotiations, the Organization for Economic Cooperation and Development (OECD) suspends negotiation on the Multilateral Agreement on Investment (MAI). The MAI would give unprecedented power to corporations, remove restrictions on the movement of capital, and allow companies to sue for lost future profits in an international mediation panel. An international coalition of more than 600 organizations from Europe, Asia, the Western Hemisphere, and spearheaded by Canada expose the secret document and derail the talks. However, the elements of the MAI are being proposed as additions to the World Trade Organization.

· Black Radical Congress. Although only 400 are expected, more than 2,000 people of African descent come to Chicago for the meeting of the Black Radical and Black Radical Feminist Congress. Recognizing contributions from diverse tendencies within Black Radicalism—including socialism, revolutionary nationalism, and feminism— the congress adopts a vision platform uniting Black radicals in opposition to all forms of oppression, including class exploitation, racism, patriarchy, homophobia, anti-immigration prejudice and imperialism.

1999 · Bolivian Popular Movement Fights for Water. The Bolivian government is forced to privatize its water system through World Bank SAPs. Bechtel takes over the service, and rates rise by 200%. A coalition of workers, environmentalists, women's groups, and peasants form under the name "Coordinadora in Defense of Water and Life." In one week of massive protest, Bechtel is forced to withdraw, and water services laws are reformed.[99]

· WTO Meeting Shut Down. At the World Trade Organization's meeting in Seattle, Washington, US activists finally join with communities in Europe, Asia, Africa and Latin America in direct action against corporate globalization & neoliberalism. During four days of intense street protest, the police, unprepared for 50-70,000 demonstrators, begin attacking demonstrators. On the final day of the Ministerial, the ministers declare the meeting a failure, and no new agreements are resolved. The victory pushes the policies of corporate globalization into the forefront of US activism.

· Puerto Rico General Strike. More than 500,000 people across Puerto Rico take to the streets for three days to protest the government's plan to privatize the national phone company.

· **Merger Mania Reaches Its Peak.** Global mergers and acquisitions reach a record, with $608 billion of total value trading hands in 9 months. Throughout the 90s banking, media & entertainment, communication and technology companies have merged, pushing the stock market up while spreading monopoly and forcing tens of thousands of workers out of jobs.[100]

2000 · SAPs Sacked & Replaced with Comprehensive Development Framework (CDF). After the Seattle protests, both the World Bank and the IMF attempt to remake their image. Structural Adjustment Programs are now called Comprehensive Development Framework, but the underlying philosophy doesn't change. Calls for meetings with non-government organizations (NGOs), poverty reduction rhetoric, and other measures are little more than public relations ploys trying to show IMF and World Bank officials as international "anti-poverty crusaders."[101]

· **Landless and Street Children's Movement organizes hundreds of land occupations in Brazil.**

· **IMF and World Bank Protests in DC.** In 1999, 25 people protest the IMF and World Bank meetings and call for cancellation of "Third World" debt. In 2000, 20-30,000 participate in three days of civil disobedience and permitted rallies. The demonstrators do not shut down the meetings, but issues of corporate globalization are kept in the spotlight.

· **World Economic Forum Protests in Melbourne, Australia.** 10,000 people protest the Asia-Pacific meeting of the World Economic Forum in Melbourne. The World Economic Forum is a 30-year old organization which serves as an international lobbying forum for corporate globalization. Although there were demonstrations at WEF meetings before, these days of protest shut down a portion of the meetings. The strategy of militant protesters - to not allow corporate globalization to conduct "business as usual" - advances.

2001 · WTO Talks in Doha, Qatar. In the first talks after the Seattle shut down, the WTO has to scale back much of its program for broad expansion. Despite growing pressure about the WTO's legitimacy, discussions by major power brokers still exclude poorer nations. The outcome of the talks is a "modest reaffirmation for on-going WTO talks on services and agriculture, agreement to start new talks on anti-dumping rules, an agreement to negotiate non-agriculture tariffs cuts which includes a US concession permitting non-reciprocal tariff cuts for developing nations and a political statement supporting interpretation of WTO rules to allow poor countries to obtain access to patented medicines."[102]

· **G8 Protests in Genoa.** As many as 300,000 people protest the G8 summit (the meeting of the 8 largest nation-state economies) in Genoa, Italy. More than 15,000 police are mobilized to control the protest on the street and another 20,000 police and troops erect a no protest zone around the actual meeting site.[103] Protester Carlo Giuliani is killed by the police sparking mass demonstrations across the world. A school serving as a refuge for protesters is raided by the police and many are beaten badly.

· **First World Social Forum (WSF) is convened in Porto, Alegre Brazil.** In opposition to the World Economic Forum held in Davos, Switzerland over 10,000 activists and organizers gather to forge relationships and discuss the possibility of another world.

· **Cuba offers 6-year medical scholarships to low-income minority students in the US.** In a speech at Riverside Church in Harlem, Cuba's Fidel Casto announced this program to be administered by the Congressional Black Congress. This program is symbolic of Cuba's ongoing efforts to forge political and economic alliances with oppressed people throughout the western hemisphere.

· **House Vote on Fast Track.** With last minute deals and arm twisting, the House of Representatives passes "fast track" legislation by one vote (215-214). The bill would grant the US President the ability to unilaterally make trade pacts. Congress could only reject or approve the deals but could make no amendments. Fast Track would further the President's push towards the FTAA (Free Trade Agreement of the Americas) and the neoliberal trend.

· **WCAR.** The World Conference against Racism, Racial Discrimination, Xenophobia, and Related Intolerance is held in Durban, South Africa. The United Nations conference is the third held on issues of discrimination and also the third the US attempts to limit, refuses to participate in, and/or withdraws from. President Bush, along with heads of some European countries, threaten to boycott the conference if reparations for slavery and colonialism are on the agenda. The US does send a low-level delegation which officially leaves the conference when delegates, particularly in the NGO forum, demand language equating Zionism with racism and discuss Israel's repression of Palestinians. In reality, the behavior is consistent with US history of undermining international conferences dealing with human rights.

· **Zapatista march to Mexico City.** After President Fox's government begins a propaganda war against the movement and refuses to uphold the San Andres accords (an agreement negotiated years earlier), the Ejercito Zapatista Liberacion Nacional (EZLN or Zapatistas) march to Mexico City. 24 delegates, including Subcomandante Marcos, cross the country and enter the city. The delegates are unarmed and accompanied by national and international civil society. National and international media attention forces Fox to make a lackluster commitment to change and allow the Zapatistas to address congress.

· **9-11: World Trade Center and Pentagon Attacks.** Four planes are hijacked and three are flown into the World Trade Center in New York City and the Pentagon in Washington, DC. The World Trade Center collapses killing thousands. As the nation mourns, the administration launches a "War on Terrorism." Basic civil liberties are undermined through such laws as the **USA PATRIOT Act** and more than 1,000 people are "disappeared" (none are charged with any crimes relating to the attacks) as the US determines the al-Qaeda network led by Osama bin Laden is responsible. Afghanistan, where bin Laden lives in exile, is invaded and the ruling party (the Taliban) are toppled. President Bush repeatedly says the war will last a long time, spread around the world, and will have no clear ending.

2001-Present · **US begins airstikes in Afghanistan on Oct. 7, signaling the beginning of War in Afghanistan.** According to Global Exchange, by December, an estimated 3,500 Afghans are killed by US bombing.

· **California Energy Crisis.** As energy prices soar in California, private industry lobbies for and receives a faulty deregulation scheme which causes

a massive energy crisis. As citizens across the state are forced to deal with timed blackouts, large energy companies like Enron use insider trading to cash in on millions.[104]

· **United Nations reports that during 2001, 3 million people died from the AIDS pandemic.** The spread of AIDS disproportionally affects the African continent, with 2.3 million of these deaths taking place in Sub-Saharan Africa.

2002 · **Euro goes into circulation.** Though in electronic circulation since 1999 the Euro goes into hard currency circulation in twelve European Union countries: Austria, Belgium, Finland, France, Germany, Greece, Ireland, Italy, Luxembourg, the Netherlands, Portugal, and Spain. National currencies are to be withdrawn from circulation by the end of February.

· **Enron Collapse.** Shadow accounting practices finally catch up with the massive energy trading conglomerate and Bush presidential campaign backer. Enron files for the largest Chapter 11 in US history. A few top-level executives are able to cash in stock options before the collapse and make millions while destroying the stock-based pensions of thousands of employees. Accounting giant Arthur Anderson is also indicted in the cover-up. As Congress and the country try to sort out what happened, Vice President Cheney refuses to release notes of meetings held with various corporate executives (including Enron) to discuss national and international energy policies.

· **Argentina meltdown.** In 1992 Argentina tied its peso to the dollar which helped reduce inflation, but causes the currency to be overvalued.[105] While other Latin American countries devalue their currency, due to IMF loan conditions Argentina cannot, and costs for its goods in other countries continues to rise. The IMF program for Argentina supports an overvalued currency while insisting on a "zero-deficit" budget despite a recession. Investors pull out and interest rates increase dramatically as soon as the IMF-supported fixed exchange rate looks like it cannot hold.[106] People across the country find they can no longer afford basic services as their earnings (in pesos) decrease in value while their bills (in US dollars) rise. In anger and despair, thousands take to the streets for weeks of protests which eventually topple 5 presidents in a row. Citizens come together in neighborhood assemblies to make decisions regarding the future of the country as well as to gather resources for immediate aid such as medical clinics and neighborhood banks. Decisions are enforced through mass demonstrations by the *piqueteros* (picketers, or unemployed) as well as mass demonstrations where participants bang on pots and pans to symbolize the lack of basic resources like food. United States does not indicate it will attempt to stabilize the situation as it did for Mexico in 1994.[107]

· **World Economic Forum Protest in New York.** As many as 20,000 people protest the international meeting of the World Economic Forum, moved from Switzerland to New York. This protest also includes a large peace demonstration, and a vision of an alternative world post 9-11. As one of the first national demonstrations since September 11th, it shows the anti-globalization movement is not dead and that militant protest is still possible and necessary.

· **US builds at least 13 new military bases after 9-11.** 50.5% of the US Budget is reserved for military spending and part of this money is used to construct military bases throughout the Middle and Near East.[109]

· **US backs attempted coup of Venezuelan President Hugo Chavez.** Although unsuccessful, the attempted coup was preceded by the "traditional hallmarks of a Washington-sponsored regime change, including increased US funding to opposition groups and high-level meetings between US officials and key people involved in the coup."[110]

· **US government announces that US troops will guard Occidental Petroleum's pipeline in Columbia.** "Plan Columbia" which backers claim is a continued effort in the War on Drugs and detractors call a Human Rights disaster, has meant billions of dollars in direct US aid, military training and weaponry to Columbia's government. This "plan" has been aggressively pushed by corporate lobbiest, including Occidental Petroleum.

· **CEOs in the United States gain a pay-increase of 178%.** In less then 10 years American CEOs make, on average, 10.3 million in annual salary.[111]

2003-Present · March 19th US-led invasion of Iraq officially begins. After a year of bombings and pre-invasion posturing the US military invasion and occupation begins.

2003 · Global Day of Protest against War. Hundreds of thousands of people protest in dozens of countries around the world on March 19th.

· **US President Bush succeeds in passing major tax cut.** The top 1% of Americans received an average $78,480 tax break while 1 in 6 American children live in poverty.[112]

· **35.9 million Americans living in poverty.** US Census reveals this increase in poverty levels to 12.5% of all Americans. Rates for people of color is higher: 24.4% for Blacks, 23.3% for Natives, and 22.5% for Latinos.

· **US President Bush announces a $15 billion dollar emergency plan in response to Global AIDS pandemic effects on Africa.** With 3.2 billion infected with AIDS in Africa many are disappointed when Bush's 'pledge' never materializes.

· **Formation of Merosur Regional Integration Bloc.** Brazilian President Lula da Silva and the new President of Argentina, Nestor Kirchner, announced their shared goal of establishing a common parliament and shared currency for Brazil, Argentina, Uruguay, Paraguay, and Associate Members Chile and Ecuador. Brazil is projecting Mercosur as the principal medium for promoting sustainable development in the region and fortifying the presence of South America on the world scene. Peru has since become a member of Mercosur, and other nations of the Andean pact (Bolivia, Colombia, Ecuador, Venezuela) are considering joining as well.

· **Iraq War begins with massive show of US military force, dropping bombs over Baghdad.** This "War" seems to announce America as a new Global Empire and has led to countless deaths and massive destruction for the people of Iraq.

· **Iran requires all European and Asian oil exports to be paid in euros instead of US dollar.**[113]

· **12 International Human Rights Organizations charge dozens of multi-national corporations with war profiteering in Congo.** In a statement to the United Nations Security Council, International Organizations such as Human Rights Watch and Oxfam appeal the Security Council to "no longer ignore clear evidence linking the exploitation of resources to the war in Congo." [114]

· **The World Trade Organization's (WTO) Fifth Ministerial Conference, Cancun, Mexico.** Talks at this important meeting collapse because of an impasse between under-developed and rich nations. A successful, united front of poorer nations stalls talks until the rich nations address their concerns.

· **Appointed ministers from 34 countries meet in Miami, Florida to discuss the Free Trade Agreement of the Americas (FTAA).** This November meeting is met with thousands of protesters who are arrested, beaten, and shot with rubber bullets by an unprecedented show of force by US police apparatus. (For more info on FTAA see glossary in this toolkit.)

· **Threat of "Big Three" US auto-makers going bankrupt shakes stock market.** General Motors (GM) loses money on every car sold and pays 16.2 billon in pensions and healthcare to current and retired employees. Historically seen as symbolic of the US national economy, many economists worry while GM stock rating is dramatically lowered to just above "junk-stock" status. [115]

2003-5 · **Grassroots Global Justice (GGJ) brings 100s of grassroots leaders to World Social Forum (WSF) in Mumbai, India.** Since 2003 GGJ, an alliance of grassroots organizations in the US, has successfully brings low income and grassroots leaders of color to the annual WSFs.

2004 · **78 million eligible voters stay home on election day in US.** In the midst of Global War and difficult financial times at home, 122 million Americans, or 60.7%, voted. However, 78 million eligible voters stayed home on Election Day. With widespread voting irregularities and charges of voter fraud, George W. Bush is again declared president. Official numbers reveal only 30.8% of eligible voters voted for Bush. [116]

· **About 4 million people killed in Congo.** The UN's International Rescue Committee reports that 3.8 million people are dead as a result of 6-year civil war.

· **China and Venezuela sign energy deal.** Venezuelan President Hugo Chavez offers China access to his country's energy sources from oil fields to direct crude oil supplies. Venezuela's largest oil market has been the United States; this deal is seen as an effort to provide much needed energy source for China while expanding Venezuela's export market. [117] China is expanding its diplomatic and economic relationship with many countries

· **Iran declares intent to set up international oil exchange dominated by Euro.** The International oil standard has always been based on the US dollar but due to a weakening dollar and hostile political posturing from the United States, Iran commits to trading oil based on euro. [118]

· **China-based company, Lenovo, purchases IBM's PC business for US$1.75 billion.** IBM, a powerful American brand and business, sells off their biggest unit to focus on global services and consulting. [119]

2005 · **Fifth annual World Social Forum.** Over 150,000 gather in Porto Alegre, Brazil to network and learn, continuing their powerful effort at bottom-up movement building.

· **2 million people incarcerated in US prisons.** After a 400% increase, the US prison populations rise past 2 million giving making it the largest penal system in the world.

· **Political and corporate elite push social security privatization.**

Citations for Bullet Point History

1 Koeller, David W. 1996-1999. "Africa South of the Sahara Chronology" North Park University. http://www.campus.northpark.edu/history/WebChron/Africa/Africa.html.

2 Ellwood, Wayne. 2001. The No-Nonsense Guide to Globalization. Oxford, UK: New Internationalist.

3 Koeller.

4 DeLong, J. Bradford. January 1997. "Slouching Towards Utopia? The Economic History of the 20th Century." University of California at Berkeley. http://econ161.berkeley.edu/TCEH/Slouch_gold8.html.

5 Polya, Dr. Gideon Maxwell. May 22, 1995. "The Forgotten Holocaust - The 1943 Bengal Famine." http://bioserve.latrobe.edu.au/about/gmp/gmp_famn.html.

6 Smith, Alan K. 1991. Creating a World Economy: Merchant Capital, Colonialism, and World Trade, 1400-1825. Colorado: Westview Press.

7 Garcia, Arnoldo & Martinez, Elizabeth. March 22, 2001. "What is Neoliberalism? A Brief Definition for Activists." CorpWatch.

8 Koeller.

9 Roberts, J.M. 1993. History of the World. New York: Oxford University Press.

10 Koeller, David W. 1996-1999. "The New Imperialism: 1800 - 1925" North Park University. http://www.campus.northpark.edu/history/WebChron/World/NewImperialsim.html.

11 Koeller.

12 Ellwood.

13 Koeller.

14 Roberts.

15 Koeller.

16 Stille, Alexander. August 11, 2001. "Globalization Now, a Sequel of Sorts." New York Times.

17 Roberts.

18 DeLong.

19 Patel, Nilesh. 1998. "The Sepoy Rebellion 1857" Emory University. http://www.emory.edu/ENGLISH/Bahri/Mutiny.html.

20 Koeller.

21 Nash, Phil Tajitsu. June 8-14, 2001. "Fifty Years Since McCarran-Walter." Asian Week.

22 Stille.

23 Stille.

24 Koeller.

25 Ellwood.

26 Nash.

27 Aronson, Goran. March 1999. "The Berlin Conference: 1884" North Park University. http://www.campus.northpark.edu/history/WebChron/Africa/BerlinConf.html.

28 Koeller.

29 Teed, Peter. 1992. A Dictionary of Twentieth Century History: 1914-1990. New York: Oxford University Press.

30 Roberts.

31 DeLong.

32 Teed.

33 Nash.

34 Teed.

35 Grabbe, J. Orlin. 1996. "The Rise and Fall of Bretton Woods" International Financial Markets, 3rd Edition. New Jersey: Prentice-Hall, Inc.

36 http://www.ilo.org.

37 Nash.

38 Teed.

39 Greider, William. 1997. One World, Ready or Not: The Manic Logic of Global Capitalism. NY: Touchstone.

40 Grabbe.

41 Nash.

42 Ellwood.

43 Teed.

44 Greider.

45 Grabbe.

46 Grabbe.

47 Grabbe.

48 Grabbe.

49 Roberts.

50 Teed.

51 Roberts.

52 Teed.

53 Nash.

54 Nash.

55 Teed.

56 Blum, William. 2000. "A Brief History of United States Interventions, 1945 to the Present." http://www.lol.shareworld.com/Zmag/articles/blum.htm.

57 Joseph, Peniel E. September 15, 2001. "Dark Days and Bright Nights: The NGO Forum of the World Conference Against Racism." Black Radical Congress. http://www.mail-archive.com/brc-news@lists.tao.ca.

58 Teed.

59 Grabbe.

60 Greider.

Project South: Institute for the Elimination of Poverty & Genocide

61 Teed.
62 Ellwood.
63 Roberts.
64 Lee, Paul. September 19, 2001. "Documents Expose US Role in Nkrumah Overthrow." Pan-African News Wire.
65 Teed.
66 Greider.
67 Greider.
68 Greider.
69 Ellwood.
70 Greider.
71 Greider.
72 Noel, Akilah F.C. "1983 United States Invasion of Grenada: National Security Threat?" http://www.mtholyoke.edu/~afnoel/grenada/grenada1.html.
73 Gonzalez, Juan. 2000. Harvest of Empire: A History of Latinos in America. New York: Viking.
74 Ellwood.
75 Greider.
76 Ellwood.
77 Teed.
78 Greider.
79 Ellwood.
80 Greider.
81 Greider.
82 Voices in the Wilderness. "Why We Are Doing This." http://www.iacenter.org/wilderns.htm.
83 Fingrut, David. 1993. "Operation Desert Storm: Outright Disinformation Scheme." Toronto http://zog.to/3/iraq-war/gulf-war.html.
84 Greider.
85 Pharr, Suzanne. 1997. Homophobia: A Weapon of Sexism. Berkeley, California: Chardon Press.
86 Greider.
87 Greider.
88 Greider.
89 Greider.
90 Caplan, Ruth. 2001. In Whose Service? GATS and the FTAA. Corton-on Hudson, NY: Apex Press.
91 Greider.
92 Caplan.
93 Greider.
94 Greider.
95 Greider.
96 Greider.
97 Nash.
98 Irish Mexico Group. 1998. "The Second Intercontinental Gathering For Humanity and against Neoliberalism"

99 Caplan.
100 Ellwood.
101 Anderson, Sarah. February 2001. "The IMF and World Bank's Cosmetic Makeover." Dollars & Sense.
102 Public Citizen. 2001. "No New WTO Round but NGO and Developing Nation Demands for WTO 'Turnaround,' Repair also Dismissed" http://www.citizen.org/trade/wto/Qatar/articles.cfm?ID=6497
103 Pandey, BB. August 2001. "Genoa Protests Against G-8 Meet." http://www.cpiml.org/pgs/partorg/liberati/2001aug/genoa.htm
104 May 8, 2001. "Energy Crisis Overview: How we got here." San Fransico Gate. http://www.sfgate.com/cgi-bin/article.cgi?file=/gate/archive/2001/05/08/lookhow.DTL
105 Weintraub, Sidney. July 2001. "The US Congress and Trade Policy: Give Me a Break." Issues in International Political Economy, Number 19. http://www.csis.org/simonchair/issues200107.htm
106 Weisbrot, Mark. "Argentina Meltdown." Dec. 2001. http://www.commondreams.org/news2001/1220-05.htm
107 Weintraub
108 World Social Forum. 2002. http://www.forumsocialmundial.org.br/eng/tseminar.asp
109 War Times September 2002
110 Weisbrot, Mark. 2003a. "Venezuela, The Other Side of the Story." International Herald Tribune.
111 White, Ben, Carrie Johnson. "Executives Cash In, Regardless of Performance. Washington Post
112 Fraser, Doug, Owen Bierber. 2004a "Election of a Lifetime". Solidarity
113 Akleh 2005
114 Lobe, Jim. 2003a. "Global Business Profit from Congo War, Groups Charge." Inter Press Service
115 Pearlstein, Steven. 2004a. "Intervention Before Bankruptcy." Washington Post
116 Faler, Brian. 2005a. "Election Turnout in 2004 Was Highest Since 1968" Washington Post
117 aljazeera.net. "China, Venezuela sign energy deal".
118 Akleh 2005
119 Denligner 2004

Workshop on *Today's Globalization*

Project South: Institute for the Elimination of Poverty & Genocide

Today's Globalization:
Workshop Narrative

Project South's Midnite School: 2005

This Workshop helps people come to a common understanding of terms causes and effects of globalization. People without any background in globalization may appreciate this workshop more than those with experience in the area. However, the Workshop and different activities in the Workshop can be altered and reshaped to fit the needs of your group, regardless of experience.

This Workshop is an outcome of Project South's work with different community-based organizations and organizing campaigns. We have seen this workshop used effectively to connect immediate issues that groups are working on locally to the issues of *Today's Globalization*. This Workshop can form a foundation for your group to have further discussions on the connections between what's going on globally and what's happening in our local communities.

Today's Globalization, and all Project South Publications depend on your feedback and evaluation so we can improve and update them. We look forward to hearing from you!

Workshop Purpose

1 To quickly review background material history, definitions, etc. of Today's Globalization.

2 To come to a common understanding of globalization's causes, its policies, and its effects.

Sample Workshop Agenda

Guidelines	**5 minutes**
Goals	**5 minutes**
Timeline Introduction & "Aha" Moment Activity	**20 minutes**
Group Discussion	**10 minutes**
Globalization Gong Show	**25 minutes**
Globalization Jeopardy	**45 minutes**
Critical Questions	**30 minutes**
Evaluation	**10 minutes**

Workshop Preparation

Facilitators should review entire workshop and plan an Agenda based on the group's needs

Facilitators should review entire toolkit to pull out resources to be used during workshop

Make flip charts in advance

Materials Needed

Globalization Glossary & Globalization Jeopardy Board

Noise-maker (Buzzer, pan & spoon, anything)

Tape, Markers, Flip Chart Paper or butcher paper

A description of each Workshop Activity: Based on the Sample Workshop Agenda

Guidelines

Purpose: Like a picture-frame, the guidelines will serve to "frame" the groups' process together during the Workshop. The guidelines should reflect the group's principles and their beliefs in how people should be with each other.

Preparation: Review "What is Popular Education" section of this toolkit and Project South's suggested guidelines.

Flow: Facilitator should go over each Guideline and explain what it means, asking for any additions. Facilitator should then get group agreement on these guidelines.

"Aha" Moment

Purpose: The timeline exercise is an interactive way to explore the history of a particular topic or issue. By incorporating participants' lived experiences with significant historical events, the timeline exercise broadens people's perspectives on the issues facing their communities. It can reveal the root-causes of an issue, and how that issue has developed over time, while helping them identify the forces that have shaped its development.

This exercise also reminds participants of past struggles for justice, the impact of those struggles, and their connection to them. This deepens participants' understandings of the issue, inspires hope based on the victories of past struggles, and lifts up valuable lessons from history. It also helps participants understand the way that economic, political, and popular movement forces affect each other and influence change.

An "Aha" Moment is a time in your life when something happened and you responded by thinking to yourself, "Aha! That's how it works!" We all have many such moments. Participants are asked to choose only one, not necessarily the first or last or most important. This exercise helps introduce people to each other and shows the level of knowledge in the room.

Although both the graphical timeline and the historical text incorporate history from all over the world, they do not reflect a world history. This toolkit was developed with educating a US constituency, and the timeline does have a US orientation.

"Aha" Moment

Preparation: Identify your workshop timeframe. You can modify your use of the timeline and other exercises depending on how much time you have. Adapt the timeline for the group, keeping your goals in mind. Project South Timelines provide a starting point and you can add events that are more geographically specific or appropriate for your particular audience. Facilitators should be familiar enough with events on the timeline to answer questions. Choose a question that will encourage the audience to share personal stories and history related to globalization, economic justice or popular movements. This question should be designed to bring forward information that will teach and engage each partici-pant personally in the workshop. If the majority are new to globalization, it's best to ask the third question since it's more open. If the majority already have some experience as activists, we suggest using the first or second.

1) "When did you first hear about globalization?"
2) "When did you first decide to work for change?"
3) "Name a time you fought for economic justice."

You should adapt the question for your audience and your specific workshop goals - appro-priate language and questions that people can relate to are keys to the success of this exercise. Reproduce the timeline in this toolkit in handout form (copy to 8.5x14 or 11x17 paper) and a wall-size version. This can be done on a self-service, oversize copy machine at a neighborhood office store.

Activity Flow: Hand out timeline & large colorful sticky notes. Ask the workshop partici-pants to put their answer to the question(s) you have chosen on the sticky note. If you

"Aha" Moment

Flow Continued:

have decided to use multiple questions, then have the participants put each answer on a different color note.

Introduce the participants to the timeline. The facilitator should lift up two major points. 1) The importance and value of looking at history. "In order to figure out where we are going, and how to get there - we have to know where we have come from. History can help us understand how the conditions we face today have developed. History teaches us that the positive things we enjoy today were won by the collective struggles of groups of 'ordinary' folks in the past."

2) We must look at history in a way that integrates economics, public policy, and popular movements. We explain that our education system often teaches us little about the inter- sections of these three areas. An explanation might include these points: "Economics is something that happens on Wall Street, or it just happens - the path of the economy is inevitable. Public policy is determined solely by our elected officials - in Congress, the state house or city hall. We are taught that public policy has little if anything to do with the economy, that they operate independent of each other. And we are usually not taught anything about popular (of the people) movements. If we are taught something, it is usu- ally about one leader or one event."

You can use an example to demonstrate the interconnection. The case of the New Deal clearly demonstrates the connection between people's movements (the strength of the labor movement and its community branches - i.e. unemployed councils) and public policy (the creation of Social Security, Aid to Dependent Children and federal job programs). And both of these forces impacted and were impacted by the economy - the Great Depression and increasing industrialization led to increased organizing, and the New Deal policies helped to improve the health of the economy. Ultimately, this time period also demon- strates the potential of people's movements to make changes against all odds. At a time when the country was broke, the federal government was forced to allocate vast resources to programs that supported people in need.

Choose the method for people to share their answers according to the size of your group and the amount of time you have. If you have a small group (or a large group with enough time) you can ask people to post their answers first, and then work your way through the answers chronologically or randomly. If you are short on time or are doing it with a really big group, ask people to pair up with someone they don't know well and share answers. Then have them come up to the wall-size timeline and post their sticky notes on the time- line in a place that fits the time and content of their answer.

Group Discussion

Purpose: Once you have covered a significant number of timeline events and participants' contributions (the number will be determined by your time restrictions), then facilitate a large group discussion about the information. The Group Discussion will give the group time to reflect on ideas that come up during that activity.

Preparation: The Group Discussion can take place while people are still standing around the timeline or participants can sit back in their seats, depending on group size and the facilitators decision.

Activity Flow: Did anything surprise you? What? How have things changed over time? What are some of the connections that you see between politics, economics, and people's movements - now and in the past? Looking at this information, what would you predict for the future? Where are we heading with regards to this issue? What lessons can we learn from the organizing work of the past? How would our organizing change if we applied these lessons?

Project South BAM: Washington, DC 2005

Globalization Gong Show

Purpose: The concept of globalization is new for many, and the language can be intimidating. Language, or being able to name things, is a form of power and this exercise helps equalize participants. The goal of the Gong Show is to insure everyone understands the terms used, not to make people feel stupid. Be sure the atmosphere is fun & focused on learning, not attacking others. Keep the workshop guidelines handy just in case.

Preparation: If all participants have little to no knowledge, pass out the glossary and ask people to study it. After a few minutes, ask people to put the glossary away and begin the game. But, if at least 1/4 of those present have some knowledge of globalization, go right into the game.

Choose some words that everyone has experience with like poverty, deregulation, downsizing, or World Bank. Before beginning, pass out noisemakers such as pots & pans, shaker, spoons, buzzers, etc. Although not everyone has to have an item, be sure that all participants can get to one easily. Once the items are distributed, explain the exercise. In 30 minutes it's possible to get through about 5 words, organizations, etc.

Workshop Flow: A word will be written on the flip chart. A volunteer will be asked to define the word in two or three sentences.

At any time during the volunteer's definition, anyone who doesn't understand or is confused by the definition must bang on the pots and pans i.e., gong.

If everyone understands the volunteer, the definition is allowed to stand and the volunteer can be given heaping mounds of candy for their effort. Only if everyone in the room understands the definition can it be allowed to stand and remain on the flip chart.

If someone disagrees with the definition, they must give their own definition again; and if people don't understand they hit the pots). If people understand, that definition also stands. Of course, there can be more than one definition of a term. This is fine. A volunteer can try again once they've been "gonged." However, try to get as many volunteers as possible before repeating.

Poor People's Day, Atlanta 2005: Education Day

Globalization Gong Show
Sample Concepts and Terms

This is a small sampling of words, concepts, terms, organizations & acronyms you can use with this exercise. You will find more definitions in the Globalization Glossary section of this Toolkit. While you should choose those that are most applicable to the participants, we highly recommend the first 9 words as very relevant to understanding today's globalization.

Poverty	**International Monetary Fund (IMF)**	**Free Trade Agreement (NAFTA)**	Privatization	Global South
Structural Adjustment Programs (SAPs)	**World Bank (WB)**	**World Trade Organization (WTO)**	Deregulation	Corporate Globalization
			Downsizing	
Neoliberalism	**General Agreement on Tariffs and Trade (GATT)**		Race-to-the-bottom	Bottom-up globalization
Free Trade Area of the Americas (FTAA)		International Financial Institutions (IFIs)	Sweatshops	Cultural Imperialism
	North American	Zapatistas	Militarism	Nationalism
			Migration	Cold War

Globalization Jeopardy

Purpose: This activity is based on the famous television show but the goal is for participants to learn more about the History, Philosophy, Institutions, and Programs involved in today's globalization. Unlike the television show, Globalization Jeopardy is played in groups and each group gets time to think about and answer questions from 4 categories. All group members should be involved and the game can be stopped if someone is confused or has a question.

Preparation: The facilitators should budget at least 20 minutes to prepare the room for the workshop. The major preparation for this activity is the creation of your Jeopardy Board before the workshop. The type of display you have is only limited by the amount of work you want to do before hand. Regardless, the most important piece of this game is to insure that participants can easily see the Categories (History, Philosophy, Institutions, Programs) and the Dollar Amounts (each of which have corresponding questions) while playing the game.

We have included two methods for creating a Jeopardy Board that both work but feel free to develop your own process.

1) Quick Preparation Version:
You will need a blank wall big enough to fit all 4 category sheets (the size of notebook paper) across and the dollar amounts (the size of note card) going down. The dollar amounts could be 100, 200, 300, 400, & 500. Make sure that each category has its own color and the dollar amounts are color-coded to match its category.

Philosophy	Institutions	Programs	History
$100	$100	$100	$100
$200	$200	$200	$200
$300	$300	$300	$300
$400	$400	$400	$400
$500	$500	$500	$500

Globalization Jeopardy
Preparation Continued:

2) Longer Preparation Version:

It should take a couple hours to build this game but once it's done you should be able to set up the game in seconds from then on. You can also create new categories and questions to do this same activity with another subject.

You will need a tri-fold piece of foam board that is 3' tall and 4' wide. This will be tall enough to fit each category across and the dollar amounts going down. You can obtain the foam board at any art or office supply store. While you can use any color, we have found that a black board shows the colors better. Lastly, you will also need 3"x5" index cards. These will be for your questions, so it's a good idea to keep many on hand.

You will need color paper of 4 different colors. Make 1 Photocopy of each category (History, Philosophy, Institutions, Programs) in a different color. Then print $100, $200, $300, $400 & $500 at the top of a separate sheet of paper for each color. Once the dollar amounts are printed fold the paper to make a pocket that will hold an index card. Write out 1 question on an index card for each dollar amount of each category. Lay everything out on the foam board to make sure there is enough room and glue it all down!

Clearly there are many ways to go about making a Globalization Jeopardy Board from the simple to complex. Be creative and feel free to redesign this game in any way to fit your group's needs. You can have surprise "Whammy's" as some of the questions, like the game show, but in any case stay focused on how your group can best learn about some of the key aspects of today's globalization.

Activity Flow: Tell Participants that this is a group exercise and all members of the team should be involved. The game can be stopped if someone is confused and has a question. Go over the purpose of the Activity.

Divide the group into at least three 3 groups of five, depending on the total number of attendees (the game goes faster with at least three groups). If you have more than 15 attendees, don't be afraid to have four or five teams. Have each group elect a spokesperson.

Once the groups are divided, pass out the Globalization Glossary. Make sure each participant has their own copy of the Glossary and explain the rules.

Globalization Jeopardy

Activity Flow Continued: The rules can be announced before the game begins.

1) Each category on the wall represents a category of globalization. Under the category are five sheets with dollar values and a question on the back of each sheet. The questions on the board do not necessarily correspond to the Globalization Glossary questions.

2) Starting from the left, each team will be asked to choose a category and a dollar value. They will be asked the question and have 10 seconds to come up with the correct answer.

3) Correct answers will be awarded the dollar value on the front of the sheet; incorrect answers will have that amount deducted from the team score. The facilitators have final say on the acceptability of an answer.

Project South BAM: Washington DC 2005

4) Each team answers one question per round. After a team answers a question, correctly or not, the next team goes. This continues until all the questions are answered.

5) Some dollar values have Whammys and each category can have one Whammy. If a team gets a Whammy they will be asked to wager up to $1000 on their ability to answer correctly. Once they wager, the facilitator should read the Whammy. A Whammy can be a question, true/false statement, or fill in the blank. Each person's life experience should be enough to give them the answer.

6) Some dollar values can also have bonus questions. Bonus questions are worth $100. An incorrect answer will not result in a penalty to the team score.

After saying the rules, begin playing Globalization Jeopardy!

Critical Questions Discussion

Purpose: Critical Questions offer participants the opportunity to consider the big picture. They are designed to help participants process the new ideas, theories, and information presented in the workshop.

Critical Questions also help us relate new information to our personal "lived" experience and continue to share that experience with other participants.

Finally, Critical Questions can be the tool that moves a group to discuss their strategy for creating change.

Preparation: As the facilitator, you should choose the questions carefully. When choosing your questions, make sure to consider the goals of the workshop, your audience and your time allotment. Choose questions that the participants can easily relate to and that will help to sum-up other information in the workshop. The questions should focus the discussion on one or two major concepts. You may need to adapt the questions that we offer in this toolkit. This discussion can last between 30 minutes and 1 hour, depending on the time and needs of your group.

Project South Vision Workshop: Incite Conference 2005

Activity Flow: Facilitator should begin by asking the group to brainstorm some answers to the questions you have prepared. The idea is to get the creative juices flowing. Then break the group into smaller groups of 4-6. Give the groups one of the questions with its brainstorm. Each small group should further discuss answers to the question and come up with either strategies for how they could change the situation in their local community or a vision of how it could be different in 50 years or more. These small groups can then choose a way to report back to the larger group. The majority of allotted time for this activity should take place in small group discussions.

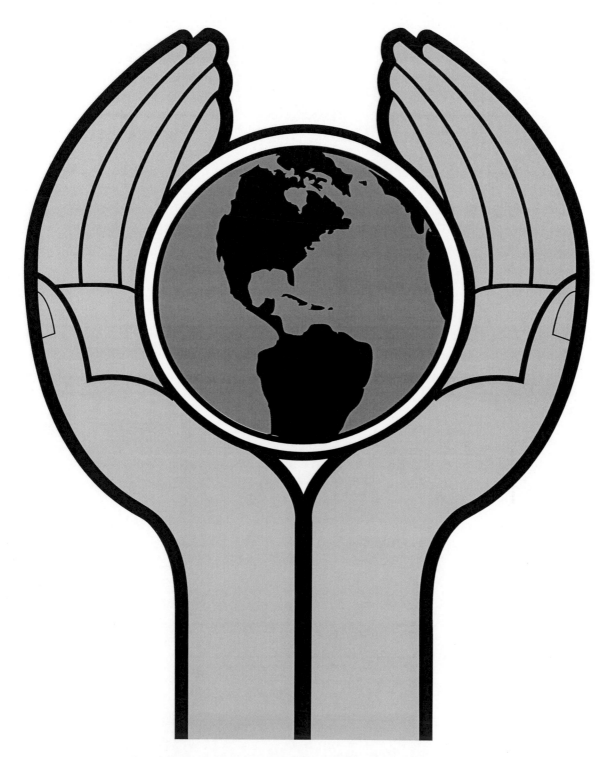

Project South: Institute for the Elimination of Poverty & Genocide

Globalization Gong Show Glossary
Economic & Political Philosophy

Globalization - An aspect of capitalism which drives expansion of the economic market system across the globe in search of maximum profits. Globalization is more than 500 years old and has run throughout the three major stages of the capitalist global economy.

Neoliberalism - Dominant set of economic & political policies guiding this stage of globalization. Founded at the University of Chicago in the late 1940's, its basic tenets are: access to free markets, privatization of government services, and deregulation.

Fast Track - aka Trade Promotion Authority. Authority given to the US President by Congress to sidestep the Constitution regarding treaty negotiation. It allows the President to negotiate a treaty always related to expanding neoliberal policies quickly by limiting Congress to a "yes" or "no" vote on the entire bill without amendment.

Race to the Bottom - Phrase used by popular movements to describe deteriorating living & working conditions of the majority of the world's population under neoliberalism. Attributes include automation, downsizing, falling wages, eroded environmental protections, contingent labor, welfare "reform", and increased global competition among workers.

Institutions

World Trade Organization (WTO) - Created in 1995 during the "Uruguay Round" of GATT negotiations, the WTO is an international organization of more than 140 countries. By targeting "non-tariff barriers to trade" like environmental, labor or safety laws), the WTO can overturn local and national laws in secret and without an appeals process.

International Monetary Fund (IMF) - Created at the Bretton Woods conference, the IMF was first mandated to regulate an international monetary system to facilitate global trade. Today the IMF now lends to countries in economic crisis & requires severe changes in economic policy including a reduced money supply & government spending, privatization, and removing restrictions on capital flows.

Prison-Industrial Complex (PIC) - Neoliberal policies, practices and institutions of all levels of government designed to remove the discarded those who are unemployable, poor, uneducated, etc.) from society to further the social control of those negatively impacted by globalization.

World Bank (WB) - Institution created at the Bretton Woods conference. Originally the International Bank for Reconstruction and Development, it was established to help finance the reconstruction of Europe after World War II and the development of poorer countries.

Globalization Gong Show Glossary

Policies & Programs

Personal Responsibility, Work Opportunity Act Welfare "Reform" - Passed & signed into law by Clinton in 1996, this ended "welfare as we knew it" & threw millions of low-income working moms into the labor market. It eliminated AFDC (Aid to Families with Dependent Children) as an entitlement, set a 5-year lifetime limit for families to receive welfare, instituted mandatory work requirements, and transferred government support to states as TANF (Temporary Assistance for Needy Families).

Structural Adjustment Programs - Policies & practices created in the 70s & 80s & forced on countries by the IMF and World Bank. Countries in economic crisis must accept a series of conditions as part of receiving international loans. These conditions - reduction of money supply, reduced government spending, privatization, and removal of restriction on capital flows - have deepened poverty, hurt the environment, and transferred wealth from developing countries in the South to industrialized countries in the North. SAPs are considered a failure and have been officially abandoned by both the IMF and the World Bank.

Comprehensive Development Framework - The "new" set of policies at the WB/IMF designed to replace SAPs. Officially it includes increased and more effective fiscal expenditures for poverty reduction with better targeting of budgetary resources, especially on social priorities in basic education and health; enhanced transparency, including monitoring and quality control over fiscal expenditures; stronger country ownership of the reform and poverty reduction process and programs, involving public participation; stronger measurable performance indicators for follow-through on poverty reduction; and, ensuring macroeconomic stability and sustainability, and reducing barriers to access by the poor to the benefits of growth. In reality, these policies are no different than SAPs.

GATT - General Agreement on Tariffs and Trade. Created in 1948 from the Bretton Woods conference, this treaty focused on promoting world trade by pressuring countries to reduce tariffs. It has formed the foundation for today's institutions like the WTO.

NAFTA - North American Free Trade Agreement. A treaty between Canada, the USA and Mexico which deregulates trade between the three also referred to as a "ménage a trade". Put into effect on January 1, 1994, NAFTA has lowered wages, as well as environmental and safety standards in each country.

MAI - The Multilateral Agreement on Investment. Referred to as "NAFTA on steroids", this treaty would have eliminated health, environment, safety & labor laws by severely limiting a country's ability to regulate trade and corporations. International grassroots pressure stopped negotiations, and the treaty was scrapped.

Globalization Gong Show Glossary

History

Bretton Woods - Conference conducted in 1944 at Bretton Woods, New Hampshire. As World War II was ending, the Western Allied countries held a conference to devise a plan for reconstructing the European economy, solidifying the US role as a superpower, countering the spread of communist ideas and enacting neo-colonial economic policies. From Bretton Woods came the IMF, the World Bank, and the General Agreement on Tariffs and Trade (GATT).

Council on Foreign Relations - Founded in 1918 as a "board of initiation." The organization was formed to foster cooperation among Western governments, international agencies, and corporations.

Trilateral Commission - Created in 1973 by economic & political elites in the US, Western Europe and Japan, the Commission coordinates & advocates corporate concerns. It serves as an international lobbying force for neoliberalism.

Stages of Economic Development - Periods of the capitalist global economy. The stages are the Mercantile, widespread agriculture and colonialism with only an early manufacturing and professional class; the Industrial/Financial, characterized by widespread use of machines in production, national markets within global production, global imperialism and division of labor; and the Electronic, the latest period of capitalist globalization which began with production increases due to greater machine use. Later period, from mid 1900's to present, has seen a breaking of the social contract and welfare state as well as low-skilled workers replaced by mechanized/robotic production and global financial institutions as the main tool of neo-colonialism and neoliberalism.

Globalization Jeopardy Questions
History

History - $100
This body, created in 1973, published a document which stated there was "too much democracy".
Answer: Trilateral Commission

History - $200
The Bretton Woods conference was held to devise a plan to do these four things; name 1.
Answers: Reconstruct the European Economy, Solidify the US role as a superpower, Counter the spread of communism and enact neo-colonial economic policies.
Bonus Question
Where is Bretton Woods?
Answer: New Hampshire

History - $300
Because of this, production has greatly increased, but many workers (particularly unskilled workers) have been pushed out of their jobs.
Answer: Use of computers in production. "Technology" also acceptable

History - $400
Beginning in 1918, this body brought Western governments and economic elites to the same table.
Answer: Council on Foreign Relations.

History - $500
Whammy
Name a past organization that fought against top-down globalization.

Globalization Jeopardy Questions

Institutions Category

Institutions - $100

When was the Multilateral Agreement on Investments (MAI) implemented?
Answer: Never. It was scrapped because of popular movement pressure in the mid-1990s.

Institutions - $200

The dolphin-safe tuna law is an example of an environmental law considered a "non-tariff barrier to trade" by this organization.
Answer: World Trade Organization (WTO)

Institutions - $300

The Zapatista Army for National Liberation (EZLN) began the modern global resistance to neoliberalism when they launched a takeover of Mexican towns on January 1, 1994 - the date this treaty went into effect.
Answer: North American Free Trade Agreement (NAFTA)

Bonus

Name a leader of the EZLN.
Answer: Examples include- Comandante Tacho, Comandante Maria, Sub-Comandante Marcos, the people

Institutions - $400

Name the 2 organizations and the treaty that came out of the Bretton Woods conference.
Answers: International Monetary Fund (IMF), World Bank & General Agreement on Tariffs and Trade (GATT)

Institutions - $500

Whammy

Give one example of people fighting globalization in your community.

Globalization Jeopardy Questions
Philosophy Category

<u>Philosophy - $100</u>
This is the birthplace of neoliberalism.
Answer: University of Chicago.

<u>Philosophy - $200</u>
This race is marked by automation, downsizing, and falling wages. Popular movements consider this the result of top-down globalization.
Answer: Race to the Bottom.

<u>Philosophy - $300</u>
How old is globalization?
Answer: 500+ years
<u>Bonus</u>
Give us an example of globalization involving Africa, Europe, and the Americas from 300 years ago.
Answer: Slavery

<u>Philosophy - $400</u>
President Clinton asked for this type of authority to negotiate the Free Trade Area of the Americas treaty or the (FTAA).
Answer: Fast track.
<u>Bonus</u>
Was he given that authority?
Answer: No

<u>Philosophy - $500</u>
<u>Whammy</u>
Give us an alternative to corporate/top-down globalization.

Project South: Institute for the Elimination of Poverty & Genocide

Globalization Jeopardy Questions

Programs Category

Programs - $100
When did Structural Adjustment Programs start?
Answer: 1970s and 1980s

Programs - $200
What three major negative consequences have resulted from SAPs?
Answers: Exacerbated poverty, greater environmental degradation, and transference of wealth from the South to the North.
Bonus
What is an example of a US SAP?

Programs - $300
What is the Comprehensive Development Framework designed to do?
Answer: Replace Structural Adjustment Programs.

Programs - $400
How long are SAPs going to officially continue?
Answer: They are considered a failure and have been abandoned.

Programs - $500
Whammy
Give us 1 example of corporate/top-down globalization having a negative effect in your community.

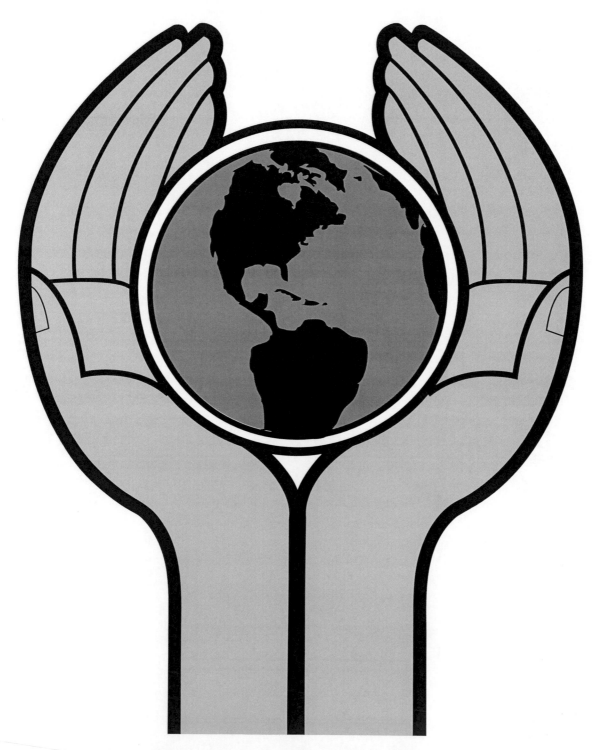

Other Resources

Project South: Institute for the Elimination of Poverty & Genocide

Project South Publications:

Project South creates various publications and popular education toolkits for community organizations, educators, facilitators, organizers, and others. All Project South publications grow from our work with various communities and community-based organizations. All publications listed below can either be purchased on our website or by contacting us by phone or mail.

Prison Industrial Complex: Social Control in the Era of Globalization
Anatomy of a Movement: The Zapatistas
The Roots of Terror
It Ain't Just About a Vote: Defining Democracy for Movement Building

Popular Education for Movement Building: A Project South Resource Guide
Volume 1 and Volume 2

Project South Workshops:

Project South calls our workshops *Building A Movement* (BAM) and the general BAM is a 2-day popular education retreat open to all educators, organizers, and community members looking for a dynamic space to discuss consciousness, vision and strategy in our growing movement. Below are some examples of workshops that can be tailored to your community's needs.

Anatomy of a Movement: Learning from History to Create the Future
Creating A Vision for Our Movement
Tree of Life
Democracy for the Few: Voting Rights Then and Now
Welfare and Jobs in the New Economy Today
Globalization: How Does It Affect You and Me?
The Changing Face of Health Care
Criminal Injustice and the Growing Police State
The Black Radical Tradition
Who's Got the Money?
The Prison-Industrial Complex: Social Control in the Era of Globalization
Globalization Hits the Hood: Gentrification in the Electronic Age

Project South: Institute for the Elimination of Poverty & Genocide

Other Popular Educators

Highlander Education & Resource Center
1959 Highlander Way
New Market, TN 37820
phone: (865) 933-3443
fax: (865) 933-3424
www.highlandercenter.org

Institute for People's Education & Action
140 Pine St., Room 10
Florence, MA 01062
phone: 413-585-8755
www.peopleseducation.org

Catalyst Centre
Suite 500 - 720 Bathurst St.
Toronto, ON M5S 2R4 CANADA
phone: 1-888-521-1453
www.catalystcentre.ca

Center for Popular Education & Participatory
Research
5501 Tolman Hall, UC-Berkeley Graduate School
of Education
phone: (510) 642-2856
www.cpepr.net

United for a Fair Economy
9 Winter Street
Boston, MA 02108
phone: (617) 423-2148
Fax: 617/423-0191
www.faireconomy.org

Applied Research Center
3781 Broadway
Oakland, CA 94611
phone: 510-653-3415
fax: 510-653-3427
www.arc.org

Teaching for Change
PO Box 73038
Washington, DC 20056
phone: (800) 763-9131
Fax 202-238-0109
www.teachingforchange.org

Community Organizations

Georgia Citizens' Coalition on Hunger
www.gahungercoalition.org

Kensington Welfare Rights Union
www.kwru.org

Southwest Organizing Project
www.swop.org

Community Voices Heard
www.cvhaction.org/

Tennessee Industrial Renewal Network
www.tirn.org   trade@tirn.org

Youth Action Research Group
http://socialjustice.georgetown.edu/research/ya
rg/

Alternate ROOTS
www.alternateroots.org/

Families & Friends of Louisiana's Incarcerated
Children (FFLIC)
www.jjpl.org

Jobs With Justice
www.jwj.org

National & Global Networks

Grassroots Global Justice Alliance
www.uevermont.org/ggj

Independent Progressive Politics Network
www.ippn.org

Sociologists Without Borders
www.sociologistswithoutborders.org

World Social Forum
www.forumsocialmundial.org.br/index.php

Project South: Institute for the Elimination of Poverty & Genocide